ENDORSE

MW00653839

There is no subject in the Bible that is more controversial and misunderstood than the Holy Spirit. The enemy has sought to keep the truths about God's Spirit hidden from the world and even the church. The reality is the Holy Spirit is God, and knowing Him intimately will empower you to walk in victory no matter what you may be facing in life.

In his new book, *Unlocking the Mysteries of the Holy Spirit*, my longtime friend and colleague, Dr. Larry Ollison, takes the truths of the Bible about the Holy Spirit and brings clarity and understanding to them in the most practical of terms. He clearly explains why we need the Holy Spirit today, what the gifts of the Spirit are and how they operate, and answers commonly asked questions people have about Him with simplicity and coherence.

God, the Holy Spirit, wants you to know Him on a deeper and more personal level. This book is designed to direct you to Him, and I am honored to highly endorse it.

Pastor Ken Blount
Ken Blount Ministries

Unlocking the Mysteries of the Holy Spirit is a clearly written, easy to understand study on the creative person of the Holy Spirit and His amazing ministry! Dr. Ollison opens up the spiritual universe and facet by facet, shines the light of disclosure on each fascinating part of His Divine personality and power. This work is fully academic, and yet, completely digestible for anyone on any level of Christian growth.

It seems that every compartment of the body of Christ has its own "twist" on the subject of the Holy Spirit. Many bend the reality of scriptural truth to suit denominational preference. However, Dr. Ollison illuminates this extremely captivating subject, not only informing, but truly inspiring the reader to become more intimately acquainted with the Holy Spirit and all He has to offer the believer.

This study unmasks the veil that "churchianity" and "selective doctrinal exposure" have thrown over this entire world of exciting revelation.

Get ready to embark upon the journey that will CHANGE YOU FOREVER!

Rev. Len Mink
Len Mink Ministries

It is with great excitement and honor that I am privileged to commend my friend, Dr. Larry Ollison, and his latest book *Unlocking the Mysteries of the Holy Spirit.*

In every era God raises up leaders to pioneer new possibilities for God's people. As Larry unlocks the attributes and benefits of the Holy Spirit, we realize the unlimited possibilities available to every believer.

In an age of religious phonies, spiritual apathy, and disheartening books, Larry unveils the truth about the Holy Spirit that brings hope and light.

If you're stuck in a religious rut, READ this book.

Rev. Barry Tubbs
Associate Minister
Kenneth Copeland Ministries

Within the person of the Holy Spirit lies the anointing. The more you and I become acquainted with the third person of the Triune Godhead the more the anointing will be released in our lives.

My good friend Dr. Larry Ollison has written a masterpiece revealing the Holy Spirit and His operation in the world today. As you read this new book, you will learn to love the Holy Spirit and have an intimate relationship with Him.

The Holy Spirit reveals Jesus and Jesus will become more real to you as you read Dr. Larry's wonderful book. I am honored to call Dr. Larry my friend and to endorse his book for the glory of God.

Dr. Gary Wood
Author of *A Place Called Heaven*

Pastor Kenneth!
Be Blessed!!
Larry Ollison

Unlocking the
Mysteries of the
Holy Spirit

DR. LARRY OLLISON

Harrison
House

Tulsa, OK

20 19 18 17 16   10 9 8 7 6 5 4 3 2 1

Unlocking the Mysteries of the Holy Spirit
ISBN 13: 978-168031053-5
Copyright © 2016 by Dr. Larry Ollison
Published by Harrison House Publishers
Tulsa, OK 74145
www.harrisonhouse.com

TABLE OF CONTENTS

INTRODUCTION

I enjoy mysteries. As a child I enjoyed stories, novels, and movies where an archeologist would discover an unknown civilization or where children would find a secret room or passageway to a special place that was undiscovered. I've always been intrigued by old castles that had secret rooms and tunnels. When I would see an old house, I would often wonder what treasures were hidden in the attic by the previous owners. I was a very curious young child.

As I grew into a young adult, the curiosity did not fade away and this curiosity extended into my spiritual life. As a young teenager in Sunday School I was the one who was always asking the questions. I remember my Sunday School teacher, who was a very nice, well-meaning deacon in the church, telling me that there are some things in the Bible that we will never know. Once I was even told, "Curiosity killed the cat," which made absolutely no sense to me whatsoever.

But I did discover this. When you ask a spiritual or biblical question and the person you are asking doesn't know the answer, you usually get an explanation that makes no sense.

The result was my curiosity about the mysteries of God was fueled all the more.

Because I was not getting any answers to my questions about the supernatural in church, I began to question other things. I became curious about the lost city of Atlantis, the pyramids, lost civilizations of giants, the Nebula of Orion, and UFOs. Of course, when you get into these things, the world is full of reputable scientists and certified goofballs who have spiritual or science fiction theories that can keep you running in circles continually.

While there was some truth and credibility in some of the knowledge I was attaining through this study, I was left with an emptiness knowing that the knowledge of man was only superficial. The more I read books and watched documentaries on these things, the more confused things became for me.

The Dream

Then one night I had a dream. In my dream I was standing in front of a brick wall. Behind me and to either side, as far as I could see, there was nothing—only a brick wall extending approximately twenty feet to my left and twenty feet to my right. At the end of each wall was another short wall of five or ten feet that took a 90 degree turn away from me and stopped. The wall was approximately twenty feet high, and from my position about ten feet away from the wall, it appeared as a brick box. There were no windows, there were no doors, there were no openings—just a solid wall with a short angled wall attached at each end.

As I stood there contemplating the wall, I noticed that on the other side of the wall there was a light that started becoming brighter. Of course, I could not directly see this light because it was on the other side of the wall. But the light radiating around the two ends and the top began to increase. Eventually the light became so extremely bright that I could see nothing. I remember trying to look at my hands, but the intensity of the light was so great that I could not even see them.

In my dream I remember thinking, "Is this what happened to Saul on the road to Damascus—a bright light that blinded him?" Then I began to realize that the light on the other side of the wall was God. The scripture came to mind—"God is light" (1 John 1:5).

Previously, I had thought if I had the opportunity, I would like to ask God about the pyramids, Atlantis, UFOs, etc. But standing there in my dream in front of the blinding light and realizing that God Almighty was on the other side of that wall, those questions dropped from my consciousness and I immediately fell to the ground.

It was as though I was clinging to the smooth, black granite floor I was prostrate on. I was desperate to humble myself before Almighty God. I wanted to get even lower than the floor. I wanted to shrink. I began to cry out and say, "Oh, God. Forgive me. I am a sinner. Oh, God. Forgive me. I am a sinner. Oh God, forgive me for I am a sinner."

The Answers

I remember screaming that out when I heard the voice of God, full of love and kindness, say to me, "Stand up, My son." As I stood there I heard Him say, "You've been asking many questions, but the answers you're longing for are really not that difficult."

Without me asking any questions, God imparted to me the answer to the lost city of Atlantis. He explained the truth about UFOs. He gave me an understanding of the giants on earth and answered the questions I had about the pyramids and all the other things I had been wondering.

I was at total peace and the answers were not difficult. I remember thinking, "Why is it that man couldn't figure this out?" The answers were so simple and understandable.

It was at that moment I woke up and when I awakened, I still had all the answers. They were very easy to understand. My first thought was to write down all the answers God had given to me. I began looking for paper and pencil, but there was none to be found in the bedroom. The answers to the questions were like several birds in a birdcage. Each bird was an answer to one of the questions, but the door to the cage was open.

I began frantically running through the house looking for paper and pen. When I found the paper, a bird flew out of the cage. I remember thinking, "I still know about the pyramids and UFOs, but I need to write these answers down! They are so simple!" I remember a thought flashed through my mind about how the world would be astonished when I explained the simplicity of these ancient truths. But when I finally found the pen and began to write, the cage was empty.

The Peace of Knowing

But I had something that I'd never had before. I had the total peace of knowing that there were answers to all these questions and that in the realm of the spirit, in God's world, these answers were so simple. And I knew that the knowledge of man, no matter how great the scientist or intriguing the theory, will always fall short to the knowledge of God.

That day I quit seeking the knowledge of man and turned all of my attention to the answers that are only revealed by the Spirit of God.

As a part of my testimony, I have shared this dream at countless meetings over the years, and I'm usually asked this question. "Why were you not able to retain the answers that God gave you?" Actually, I believe I have retained them. They are in my spirit and because of this, I am not concerned about the answers.

While these subjects are still interesting, they are no longer consuming because I know they are a part of the knowledge of the Spirit. With that knowledge in my spirit, I can now explore even deeper mysteries in the Word. While soulish mysteries are interesting, if we allow them to consume us, they will hinder us from the deep things of God that are only revealed by the Holy Spirit.

But God has revealed them to us through His Spirit. For the Spirit searches all things, yes, the deep things of God.

1 Corinthians 2:10

CHAPTER 1

THE REVELATION OF THE HOLY SPIRIT

In the beginning God created the heavens and the earth. The earth was without form, and void; and darkness was on the face of the deep. And the Spirit of God was hovering over the face of the waters.

Genesis 1:1-2

The beginning of time recorded in Genesis 1:1 is the marker or starting point for the time of man and for our historical knowledge. However, we must remember this is not the starting point for God. God has eternally existed and because of this, it is impossible to compile God's historical past. No matter how far you reach into His past, you will never find His beginning, because there is none.

Because man was created and placed on a planet that had a limited amount of land and air and because man separated himself from God through sin, the understanding and comprehension of the human mind is limited. Man sees everything with a beginning and an end. The sun rises in the morning and sets in the evening. Man departs from a destination and arrives at his destination. Mankind experiences birth and death. Simply put, it is impossible for the mind of man to comprehend an existence without beginning or end.

To attempt to explain the history of God before He stepped into darkness and said, *"Let there be light,"* would be futile. Only when we move into the eternal kingdom, with our resurrected, glorified bodies and experience the limitlessness of time and eternity, will we begin to understand the vastness of God.

The Trinity

The Spirit of God is God. While the Scripture tells us that God exists as the Father, the Word, and the Holy Spirit, we must fully understand that these three are one. As Christians, we do not worship multiple gods, but rather we worship one God. As Christians, we are monotheistic. We worship Jehovah God—the God of Abraham, Isaac, and Jacob—who has always been and shall always be (Revelation 1:8). He is without beginning and without end. He created man on the sixth day and in the days of man on the earth, God has revealed Himself to us in three distinct ways: God the Father, God the Son, and God the Holy Spirit (1 John 5:7).

While the word trinity is not in the Bible, the concept is woven throughout the Scriptures. The Bible clearly teaches that God functions in three different manifestations and this allows us to understand the completeness of Almighty God.

Through the years, there have been attempts to illustrate how God could be three and still be one. One illustration is that of water (H_2O). Water can be ice, it can be liquid, and it can be vapor. It can freely move between these three forms without changing what it is. While one person may see ice, in another place a person may see steam, while another sees water.

In some cases, all three manifestations can be seen at once. My house overlooks the Lake of the Ozarks and sometimes in the winter, the lake will freeze over. When spring arrives, the ice melts on top and early in the morning you can see steam rising. In other words, you can see ice, water, and steam at the same time.

Another illustration is of a man who is a father, a husband, and a son. Who you are affects how you see the man. To his father, he's a son. To his wife, he is a husband, and to his children, he is a father. But at the end of the day, he is still the same person and all three are one.

While these illustrations show the possibility of three being one and one being three, they still fall short of the magnitude and complexity of God Almighty. Let's take a look at a few of the scriptures where God reveals Himself.

Father, Son, and Holy Spirit

In the beginning God revealed Himself as the Creator where the Bible says God created the heavens and the earth (Genesis 1:1). Then we discover His Spirit hovered over the face of the waters on the earth (Genesis 1:2) revealing His power and oversight of the creation. We also know the Word of God (later revealed as Jesus in John 1:14) was present at the time of creation also. In fact, Jesus, the Word of God, created

Voice Activated

everything that God the Father spoke. Through the Word, Jesus created all that is seen in the universe for Himself.

> **For by Him all things were created that are in heaven and that are on earth, visible and invisible, whether thrones or dominions or principalities or powers. All things were created through Him and for Him.**
>
> Colossians 1:16

So here we can clearly see the concept of the trinity at the very onset of the Bible. Throughout the Bible, it is undeniable that the Father, Son, and the Holy Spirit were present at the creation of the universe in which man now exists and that the Father, the Word, and the Holy Spirit are one.

Although God the Father sent His Son (Jesus, the Word) to the earth and although the Spirit of Almighty God the Father, the Holy Spirit, lives in every born-again believer, the Father, the Son, and the Spirit together make one God—inseparable.

In Luke, we are told the Holy Spirit came upon a young girl named Mary and she conceived and bore a Son (Luke 1:31). Of course, that Son was Jesus. When Jesus prayed to God, He referred to Him as His Father. Since the Father is the one who impregnated the mother of Jesus (Mary), then obviously the Holy Spirit and the Father are one.

Remember Jesus told His disciple, Philip, that if he would look at Him, he would actually be seeing the Father because He and the Father were one (John 14:8-11).

Of course, the Spirit of God is God in the same way your spirit is you. In fact, you could say your spirit is the real you.

When Jesus referred to His Father in heaven, He did not separate the Holy Spirit from Him. So if Jesus and the Father are one, and the Father and the Holy Spirit are one, then the only conclusion is this: The Father, the Son, and the Holy Spirit, these three are one (1 John 5:7).

When Jesus was 30 years old, He was baptized in the Jordan River. As He came out of the water, there was a voice that came from Heaven. It was clearly the voice of God and He said, "This is My beloved Son, in whom I am well pleased" (Matthew 3:17).

When Jesus sent out His disciples and gave them the command to evangelize the world, He said they should teach all nations and baptize the believers in the name of the Father and of the Son and of the Holy Spirit (Matthew 28:19). He was clearly showing the three manifestations of God.

Jesus made another interesting statement in John 8:58 when He stated that, "Before Abraham was, I AM." Once again, He clearly stated that even though He was the Son of Man on earth, He Himself was also God Almighty.

There are dozens of other proofs in the Scripture, but they can all be summed up clearly in this one verse. First John 5:7 says, "There are three that bear witness in heaven: the Father, the Word, and the Holy Spirit; and these three are one." These three are what we refer to as the trinity.

The Manifestation of the Holy Spirit

Noah Webster's 1828 Dictionary describes manifestation as *"the act of disclosing what is secret, unseen or obscure; discovery to the eye or to the understanding; the exhibition of any thing by clear evidence; display; as the manifestation of God's power in creation, or of His benevolence in redemption."* In other words, when something is manifest, it can be seen and experienced.

God has chosen to manifest Himself on this earth through His Holy Spirit in many ways. The Holy Spirit moves inside of those who receive Jesus as their Lord and Savior and He lives there in His fullness. The Holy Spirit has characteristics that are described as the fruit of the Spirit and He does the work of the Father through the believer through guidance, instruction, and revelation and through nine spiritual gifts.

The Holy Spirit is omnipresent. That means He can be in multiple places at the same time and in each place manifesting Himself as He desires.

Later in this book, we will examine in detail the gifts of the Spirit, the fruit of the Spirit, and the way He leads the believer to a life of victory. But before we do that, let's take a closer look at God's plan for His Spirit on the earth.

Seeing the Unseen

While we do not look at the things which are seen, but at the things which are not seen. For the things which are seen are temporary, but the things which are not seen are eternal.

2 Corinthians 4:18

The world was created temporal by the Word of God as a place for man to exist and have dominion forever. This physical world is considered temporary by God, but He considers the unseen world of the spirit as eternal. He is the Creator who, by His Word, spoke everything we see into existence. If man could travel at the speed of light, which is 186,282 miles per second, or 670,616,629 miles per hour, it would take billions of years to travel to the galaxies we now see with telescopes in space and observatories. Truly the vastness of the creation we can see is beyond our imagination, but it pales in comparison to what we can't see.

While the Scriptures clearly tell us that God created everything both visible and invisible (Colossians 1:16), we are also instructed in the Scriptures to walk by faith and not by sight (2 Corinthians 5:7). In other words, the things of the Spirit that are unseen are more reliable and true than what you see and sense with your natural senses. One of the great purposes of the Holy Spirit for mankind is to draw, guide, reveal, and seal us so that we can be transformed and delivered from darkness into the kingdom of light, which is spiritual and eternal.

When Paul was writing to the Corinthians, he made a statement that is often quoted. He said, *"Eye has not seen, nor ear heard, nor have entered into the heart of man the things which God has prepared for those who love Him"* (1 Corinthians 2:9). While this is an eloquent, much quoted phrase, Paul is actually revealing a deep truth of the spirit realm. He is saying that your eyes cannot see and your ears cannot hear and your heart cannot imagine the things of the spirit realm.

But he goes on to say God has miraculously revealed them to those who are believers through His Spirit and it is the

Spirit who searches the deep things of God (1 Corinthians 2:10). He strongly implies that without the Spirit, the senses of man and the heart of man would never be able to detect these things. It is the Spirit of God that brings revelation and without the Spirit, there is no revelation of the spirit world.

Because the deep things of God that are unseen to man in the spirit world are only revealed by the Holy Spirit, the natural world on this earth is confused and does not understand when the things of the Spirit are explained to them in a natural, intellectual way. In Paul's letter to the Corinthians, he told them the natural man cannot receive the things of the Spirit of God because they are foolishness to him; there is no way that they can know the things of the Spirit, because they are spiritually discerned (1 Corinthians 2:14).

Seeing Into the Spirit World

In Second Kings 6, the king of Syria declared war upon Israel. However, when the king of Syria planned his attacks, Israel was forewarned and avoided the battle. This happened so consistently that the king of Syria thought he had a spy within his own camp. But upon investigation, he discovered he did not have a spy in his camp, but instead the prophet Elisha was telling the king of Israel the secret plans of the Syrians. Elisha was prophesying by the direction of the Holy Spirit and telling the king of Israel things he could never have otherwise known.

The king of Syria commanded his troops to find Elisha. They found the prophet in Dothan, so the king sent horses and chariots and a great army there. They traveled secretly by night and as the sun rose, this great army could be seen all around the city. Early that morning, the servant of Elisha was awakened to the sight and sounds of a great army prepared for war, surrounding the city of Dothan. Of course, the servant of the prophet was very upset and exclaimed, "Master, what shall we do?" Elisha answered him and gave him instruction that would seem foolish if he was only looking at the circumstances. He said, *"Do not fear, for those who are with us are more than those who are with them"* (2 Kings 6:16).

To the servant, this must have sounded ridiculous because there were thousands ready for battle all around the city. As far as he could see, there were only two—Elisha and himself—to stand against this great army.

Elisha was not young in faith, but instead was seasoned in the things of God and sensitive to the Spirit of God. He had learned the power of God is not diminished because of the great appearance of the enemy. Instead of reacting by what he saw and stepping into fear, he acted upon the Word of God and stepped into faith. Elisha prayed and said, "Lord, open the eyes of this young man that he may see" (v. 17). The Lord immediately answered the prayer of Elisha and opened the young man's eyes so he could see the seen and the unseen. What he saw was the great and full army of the Lord, horses, and chariots of fire surrounding Elisha.

As the story continues, the Syrians were struck with blindness (v. 18) and the story ends with victory. However, the point is this. The great and mighty army of God did not arrive when Elisha prayed. The army of God was already there; it was just invisible. When Elisha prayed, the young man's eyes were opened and he was able to see what had been there all along.

Many times in life, we look at the circumstances and see the great army of the enemy stationed in battle array ready to come against us. But we should never underestimate the great and mighty army of God. Although it may not be seen, it is still there and it has greater strength than the enemy. When we walk by faith and base our actions upon what God says instead of walking in fear with our actions based upon the appearance of the enemy, then the power of God will be manifested and we will see victory.

We Live in a Sensory World

The natural world is led by sight. People commonly say, "I'll believe it when I see it." Unfortunately, many in the church are led by sight. Even though they are born again, love God, and have eternal life, many miss blessings on the earth because their decisions and actions are determined by what they see.

God's Word contains promises to the believer. However, these promises are not automatically obtained. There are those who live on the earth who have an entitlement mentality. While the Word says if you don't work, you don't eat (2 Thessalonians 3:10), there are people who believe that food, clothing, and housing should be given to them simply because they exist. This entitlement mentality has crept into the church and many feel the blessings of God are automatic.

Just because they are a believer, they feel they should walk in the full blessing of God.

However, while we are living under grace and our salvation is totally determined by receiving the work of Jesus and His sacrificial blood on the altar, our blessings are conditional. Jesus said if you first seek the kingdom of God and if you seek His righteousness, then all these things will be added unto you (Matthew 6:33). Jesus said if you speak to the mountain (take authority), then the mountain will move (Mark 11:23). We are told in the Scriptures that a principle of faith is to call things that are not (seen) as though they are (Romans 4:17).

However, these conditions cannot be met if you totally rely on your earthly vision. You must see your need met, you must see the mountain moved, you must see the blessing (with your spiritual eyes). This can only be done by believing what God's Word says about the unseen, rather than believing your own physical eyes. We access the physical world with the five physical senses, but we access the spiritual things of God through the realm of the spirit.

God is Spirit, and those who worship Him must worship in spirit and truth.

John 4:24

Before we can attain greater revelation concerning the Holy Spirit, we must establish some foundational principles. Without these principles, it is impossible to understand how we interact with the spirit world and grasp the revelation of why things happen.

Foundational Principles

Throughout the centuries, the church has been divided because of doctrine. The word "doctrine" comes from the Greek word *didaché* which simply means teaching. Wrong doctrine or teaching has kept the church divided.

Most wrong teaching comes from the lack of knowledge of the Word, and some comes from the confusion that results from listening to the doctrines of demons (1 Timothy 4:1). However, one thing is for sure. Unless you allow the Holy Spirit to give you revelation on these basic fundamental truths, your understanding of the Bible will be skewed.

Here are the foundational principles:

- Man is a three-part being—spirit, soul and body.
- Righteousness and holiness are not the same.

Man Is a Three-Part Being

Now may the God of peace Himself sanctify you completely; and may your whole spirit, soul, and body be preserved blameless at the coming of our Lord Jesus Christ.

1 Thessalonians 5:23

You must know you are a three-part being—spirit, soul, and body. They are three distinct, different Greek words—spirit (*pneuma*), soul (*psuche*), and body (*soma*). One way of saying it: you are a spirit, you live in a body, and you possess a soul.

You were created in the likeness and image of God. God is a three-part being—Father, the Word (Jesus), and Spirit (1

John 5:7). In the same way that it is impossible to understand the Holy Bible without understanding that God is Father, Word, and Spirit, it's likewise impossible to understand the things of the Spirit without knowing that man is spirit, soul, and body.

Spirit, Soul, and Body

We are confident, yes, well pleased rather to be absent from the body and to be present with the Lord.

2 Corinthians 5:8

Spirit—Your spirit is the real you. When you receive Jesus Christ as your Lord and Savior, it is your spirit that is born again. At that moment, old things pass away and all things become new. When you receive salvation, you become a new creation. The Spirit of God moves inside of your spirit to live—not just to visit, but to live. Your everlasting life begins at that moment. Your spirit will live for all eternity. Your death is recorded on the cross of Jesus (Romans 6:6). Death is now in your past and no longer in your future.

Whoever lives and believes in Me shall never die.

John 11:26

Soul—Your soul is your mind, your will, your intellect, and your emotions. Your soul is where decisions are made on what you think and what you do. Your soul must decide whether to be led by the flesh or to be led by the Spirit. Depending upon what your soul decides, your body will respond.

Body—As a Christian, your body is the temple of the Holy Spirit. Not only is your own spirit contained within your body, but the Holy Spirit also lives within your spirit from the day of your salvation. Your body, while on the earth, is not eternal and it will eventually die and decay. It is like your earth suit. In the same way an astronaut can only live in space with a space suit, your spirit can only stay on earth with an earth suit. An astronaut can't live in space if his space suit is destroyed, and you cannot remain on earth if your body is destroyed. When your body dies, your spirit must depart (James 2:26).

When you receive Jesus as your Lord and Savior, it is your spirit that is born again, not your body. Your body will be glorified in the future, but that does not happen until the rapture of the church.

Righteousness and Holiness Are Not the Same

Simply put, righteousness is what God does for you and holiness is what you do for God. Righteousness is a result of your accepting His work and holiness is a result of Him accepting your works. Let me explain.

Under the New Covenant, anyone who believes that God raised Jesus from the dead and confesses Him as Lord is saved (Romans 10:9). At the moment that a person chooses to believe and confess Him, a supernatural miracle takes place. Old things pass away (sin) and all things are made new. This person becomes a new creation (or creature or new person) (2 Corinthians 5:17). Their spirit is born again.

At this point, this born-again person is cleansed from all unrighteousness. If they are cleansed from all unrighteousness, how much unrighteousness do they have? None! They are totally cleansed.

At salvation, the Spirit of God moves inside of the new believer to live forever. Everlasting spiritual life begins. The newly-reborn spirit is possessed by the Spirit of God and sealed by the Holy Spirit Himself until the day of redemption (Ephesians 4:30).

God is light and no darkness can enter into Him (1 John 1:5). That's why a Christian cannot be possessed by an unclean spirit. They already have the Spirit of God within them. The reborn Christian's body becomes the home of the Holy Spirit and He does not share His home with demonic spirits.

> **Do you not know that your body is the temple of the Holy Spirit who is in you, whom you have from God, and you are not your own?**
>
> **1 Corinthians 6:19**

> **Whoever has been born of God does not sin, for His seed remains in him; and he cannot sin, because he has been born of God.**
>
> **1 John 3:9**

Because we have the understanding that man is spirit, soul, and body, we can see how the spirit is cleansed and does not sin, while the flesh (body) is still subject to the temptations and addictions of the world.

Paul said a war was taking place between his spirit and his flesh. While our spirit man is righteous, our flesh must be brought into subjection and become holy.

> **For the flesh desires what is contrary to the Spirit, and the Spirit what is contrary to the flesh. They are in conflict with each other, so that you are not to do whatever you want.**
>
> **Galatians 5:17 (NIV)**

As a Christian matures through the daily meditation on the Word, holiness is increased. However, you are never any more righteous than the day of your salvation. Righteous is what you are. Holy is what you become.

Righteousness is established and is constant. Holiness increases through obedience. We are saved by grace through faith (Ephesians 2:8). We become holy by obedience that activates the grace of God and empowers us to do His will.

Righteousness is a condition of the born-again spirit of man and holiness is the conscious submission of the flesh to the will of God.

Understanding the Truth

As we read, study, and meditate on God's Word, His Spirit will reveal mysteries that have been hidden through the ages until these last days.

> **God, who at various times and in various ways spoke in time past to the fathers by the prophets, has in these last days spoken to us by His Son.**
>
> **Hebrews 1:1-2**

Throughout eternity past, God established His Word. While God has not changed and neither has His Word, the revelation of His purpose for mankind has been progressive. But in these last days, His Word has been and is being revealed to a greater depth and understanding of the truth by the Holy Spirit.

As we explore the work of the Old Testament saints, we can see the plan of God unfolding and moving toward completion in His Son, Jesus Christ.

CHAPTER 2

THE HOLY SPIRIT IN THE OLD TESTAMENT

Create in me a clean heart, O God, and renew a steadfast spirit within me. Do not cast me away from Your presence, and do not take Your Holy Spirit from me.

Psalm 51:10-11

King David was a musician and he was quite literally a psalmist. From his heart and through the inspiration of the Holy Spirit, he wrote songs that were sung to God by the nation of Israel. In his life he had experienced the Holy Spirit coming upon him and guiding him to victory. Likewise, he had experienced times of the absence of the Holy Spirit in his life. If ever there was a biblical example of someone who had experienced the presence and experienced the absence of the Holy Spirit, it was King David.

In his song that is recorded in Psalm 51, his heart cries out to God with a desire for purity of spirit. His heart cried out that the Holy Spirit would not depart from him. How could this be? How could a man who had been anointed to be king of Israel at an early age by the prophet of God, through the guidance of the Holy Spirit, experience the presence and absence of the Holy Spirit to such an extent that he would cry out for the Spirit to not depart?

Prophets, Priests, and Kings

While the question may seem complex, the answer is very basic and fundamental. King David was living under the Old Covenant that existed before God sent His Son to the earth. Under the Old Covenant, the Holy Spirit came upon prophets, priests, and kings for a specific purpose. Some were even filled with the Holy Spirit; however, none of these visits were permanent.

It wasn't until Jesus placed His blood on the altar in heaven on the day of His resurrection that a way was made for the Holy Spirit to live permanently inside of everyone who believed. Until that moment, the Holy Spirit only visited the prophets, priests, and kings for a purpose. But now, because of the precious blood of Jesus, all who believe are priests and kings in the kingdom of God (Revelation 1:6) and the Holy Spirit lives inside of each one permanently—for all eternity (John 14:16). While the Old Testament believers received a visitation, the New Testament believers receive a habitation. He visited them, but He lives in us!

But now He has obtained a more excellent ministry, inasmuch as He is also Mediator of a better covenant, which was established on better promises. For if that first covenant had been faultless, then no place would have been sought for a second.

Hebrews 8:6-7

The Spirit of Grace

The ministry of the Holy Spirit under the Old Covenant was not the same as it has been since the day Jesus placed His blood on the altar in heaven. However, from the day of creation until that day, the Holy Spirit was active on the earth in the lives of the Old Testament saints.

While grace (which is the power of God that saves us through our faith in Him) is a New Testament teaching, the grace of God was poured out in abundance before Jesus placed His blood on the altar.

Enoch walked with God and God took him (Genesis 5:24). He did not face death. Noah, a Gentile, was chosen by the grace of God to preach deliverance (2 Peter 2:5) and God saved him, his wife, his three sons and their wives from destruction. Rahab, the harlot, hid the spies and she and her family were not killed (Hebrews 11:31).

It is evident in the Scriptures that these people had faults. But God is a God of love and has sought to deliver His creation from destruction. His grace and mercy has no boundaries. By His own Word, His mercy endures forever (Psalm 107:1).

33

God Has Not Changed

After the law was given to Moses on Mt. Sinai, the Spirit of God dwelt inside the ark of the covenant. The ark of the covenant was placed in the tabernacle and later in the temple and from there the priests would minister to the people. God's presence was greatly determined by their obedience and as they refused to reverence God, the glory of God departed (Ezekiel 10:18).

While the Bible says God has not changed (Malachi 3:6), some may ask this question. Why does it seem like there is such a contrast between how God dealt with His people in Old Testament times and how graciously He deals with the church in New Testament times?

In Old Testament times, it seems that God was hard-hearted when dealing with His people and removed His Holy Spirit because of their disobedience, while in New Testament times we are told He is the God of love who seals us by His Holy Spirit until the day of redemption, and that His Spirit abides within us forever. While God does not change, why does it seem like, to some, that He's had a shift in His personality and attitude? The answer is the blood of Jesus.

Because man placed his belief in the words of Satan instead of the Word of God in the Garden of Eden, man separated himself from the presence of God. By doing this, he also separated himself from personal communion with God and His protection.

But when the perfect sacrificial Lamb (Jesus) placed His blood on the altar in heaven on the day of His resurrection, a paradigm shift took place and man could once again have intimate fellowship with God by receiving the work of the blood through Jesus. While God seemed distant in Old Testament times, it was actually because man had distanced himself from God and, because of sin, could not draw near to the Father. The sin that was brought into the world by the first man (Adam) was removed by the second man (Jesus).

For as by one man's disobedience many were made sinners, so also by one Man's obedience many will be made righteous.

Romans 5:19

So the conclusion is this. The loving God of the ages has never changed. It was man that changed. To say that the God of the Old Testament was cruel, while the God of the New Testament is love, is a feeble attempt to blame God for the sin of man.

Old Testament Examples

The following are some examples of the Holy Spirit empowering people in the Old Testament.

Joseph—While the world was living under the bondage of sin, Pharaoh recognized the Spirit of God was in Joseph (Genesis 41:38).

Balaam the Prophet—*"Balaam raised his eyes, and saw Israel encamped according to their tribes; and the Spirit of God came upon him"* (Numbers 24:2).

Othniel the Son of Kenaz—*"When the children of Israel cried out to the Lord, the Lord raised up a deliverer for the children of Israel, who delivered them: Othniel the son of Kenaz, Caleb's younger brother. The Spirit of the Lord came upon him, and he judged Israel..."* (Judges 3:9-10).

Gideon—*"But the Spirit of the Lord came upon Gideon; then he blew the trumpet, and the Abiezrites gathered behind him"* (Judges 6:34).

Jephthah, a Mighty Man of Valor—*"Then the Spirit of the Lord came upon Jephthah, and he passed through Gilead and Manasseh, and passed through Mizpah of Gilead; and from Mizpah of Gilead he advanced toward the people of Ammon"* (Judges 11:29).

Samson—The Spirit empowered Samson: *"And the Spirit of the Lord began to move upon him at Mahaneh Dan between Zorah and Eshtaol"* (Judges 13:25).

The Spirit later left Samson: *"...So he awoke from his sleep, and said, 'I will go out as before, at other times, and shake myself free!' But he did not know that the Lord had departed from him"* (Judges 16:20).

King Saul—The Spirit of God came upon King Saul: *"When they came there to the hill, there was a group of prophets to meet him; then the Spirit of God came upon him, and he prophesied among them"* (1 Samuel 10:10).

But later the Spirit left him: *"But the Spirit of the Lord departed from Saul..."* (1 Samuel 16:14).

King David—*"Then Samuel took the horn of oil and anointed him in the midst of his brothers; and the Spirit of the Lord came upon David from that day forward"* (1 Samuel 16:13).

Azariah—*"Now the Spirit of God came upon Azariah the son of Oded"* (2 Chronicles 15:1).

Daniel—*"But at last Daniel came before me (his name is Belteshazzar, according to the name of my God; in him is the Spirit of the Holy God)..."* (Daniel 4:8).

"There is a man in your kingdom in whom is the Spirit of the Holy God. And in the days of your father, light and understanding and wisdom, like the wisdom of the gods, were found in him; and King Nebuchadnezzar your father—your father the king—made him chief of the magicians, astrologers, Chaldeans, and soothsayers" (Daniel 5:11).

Joshua—*"And the Lord said to Moses: 'Take Joshua the son of Nun with you, a man in whom is the Spirit, and lay your hand on him'"* (Numbers 27:18).

Bezalel—*"Then the Lord spoke to Moses, saying: 'See, I have called by name Bezalel the son of Uri, the son of Hur, of the tribe of Judah. And I have filled him with the Spirit of God, in wisdom, in understanding, in knowledge, and in all manner of workmanship'"* (Exodus 31:1-3).

Through these and many more examples, God imparted His Spirit to mankind in ages past for the end purpose of the revelation of His Son. God's plan and purpose before the cross is the same as His plan and purpose after the cross. Although His creation separated itself from the Creator by sin, He has reconciled back to Himself all who would repent and come home.

Like the prodigal son that left the Father's house, God the Father stands waiting for His repentant sons to come home. When they do, their disobedience is washed away and they are rewarded with robes and are sons forever as though the disobedience had never occurred.

The Blessing on Abraham's Seed

Abram was a Gentile living in a pagan country when God called him out of the land of Ur and blessed him. Because of Abram's faith and obedience, God made him the father of many nations and promised to bless the world through his seed. (Genesis 12:1-3.)

Today the nation of Israel (Abraham's seed) continues to bless the world through scientific inventions and medical discoveries unlike any other nation on earth. Likewise, in this current dispensation, the world is to also be blessed by the church because those who accept Jesus as their Lord and Savior are also Abraham's seed and heirs according to the promise.

> **And if you are Christ's, then you are Abraham's seed, and heirs according to the promise.**
>
> **Galatians 3:29**

The blessings and the gifts to the church under the New Covenant are anchored in the promises of the Old Covenant.

CHAPTER 3

JESUS AND THE HOLY SPIRIT

The Spirit of the Lord is upon Me, because He has anointed Me...

Luke 4:18

After Mary, the mother of Jesus, was betrothed to Joseph, but before they had marital relations as husband and wife, she was found to be pregnant by the Holy Spirit. Her husband, Joseph, was a good man and did not want to bring public disgrace to her. He had thought of a plan to secretly put her away. But while he was making his plans, an angel of the Lord appeared to him in a dream and told him he should not be afraid to complete the marriage with Mary as his wife, because the conception inside of her was of the Holy Spirit. (Matthew 1:18-20.)

After receiving this dream, he did as the angel of the Lord commanded him to do and he took Mary as his wife, but he did not have physical relations with her until after the birth of her Son, Jesus. The seed placed in Mary's womb was not seed from her husband, Joseph, but from the Holy Spirit. While the virgin birth is defined by the reality that she did not have sexual relations with a man before having a child, the truth is still evident that a seed was placed within her womb, because conception took place.

A Virgin Mother and a Heavenly Father

The Bible tells us that life is in the blood (Leviticus 17:11) and because the mother of Jesus was a virgin and His Father was heavenly, His conception was unlike that of any other man on earth.

> **Therefore, just as through one man sin entered the world, and death through sin, and thus death spread to all men, because all sinned—**
>
> **Romans 5:12**

The Bible tells us that God has made from one blood all the nations of the earth (Acts 17:26). Because of the sin of Adam, sin was transmitted to all mankind. This is why no man—Enoch, Noah, Moses, Abraham, Elijah—none of these great men of God could save the world. No matter how hard they tried, no matter what sacrifice they made, and regardless of their obedience, their blood would never measure up to the standard of perfection required to complete the plan of salvation for man (Hebrews 9:13-14). All of the fathers of these great men were earthly. Their lineage was from Adam and therefore their blood was tainted with sin.

While the mother of Jesus was earthly, His Father was heavenly and therefore His lineage was from above. Because the Father provided the seed at conception by way of His Holy Spirit, the blood of Jesus was different from the blood of any other human on earth, and the only blood acceptable for the altar in heaven.

This is why it was so important for Jesus to finish the work He was sent to do. Had He yielded to temptation and sinned, there would have been no purpose in His resurrection. He was the only hope for the salvation of mankind.

> **For we do not have a High Priest who cannot sympathize with our weaknesses, but was in all points tempted as we are, yet without sin.**
>
> **Hebrews 4:15**

The Baptism of Jesus

> **It came to pass in those days that Jesus came from Nazareth of Galilee, and was baptized by John in the Jordan. And immediately, coming up from the water, He saw the heavens parting and the Spirit descending upon Him like a dove. Then a voice came from heaven, "You are My beloved Son, in whom I am well pleased."**
>
> **Mark 1:9-11**

John the Baptist and Jesus were related. The Bible says Mary, the mother of Jesus, and Elizabeth, the mother of John, were relatives (Luke 1:36). John baptized and preached repentance for the remission of sins. People from the land of Judea and even from Jerusalem followed his teachings and were baptized in the Jordan River.

In his preaching, John would say there was someone coming after him who was greater than himself and who would baptize with the Holy Spirit and fire (Matthew 3:11). On the Day of Pentecost this happened as the young church was baptized with fire when they received the Holy Spirit in the upper room.

> **Then there appeared to them divided tongues, as of fire, and one sat upon each of them.**
>
> **Acts 2:3**

It was during this time of John's ministry that Jesus came from Nazareth of Galilee and John baptized Him in the Jordan River. As Jesus came out of the water, the heavens opened and the Holy Spirit descended upon Jesus like a dove (Matthew 3:16). A dove is the symbol used by artists throughout the centuries to depict the Holy Spirit. However, the Bible is speaking figuratively and not literally. The Holy Spirit descended upon Him gently, like a dove.

As the Holy Spirit descended upon Jesus, a voice came out of heaven. It was the voice of Almighty God speaking to His only begotten Son and the voice said, *"You are My beloved Son, in Whom I am well pleased"* (Mark 1:11).

Strength to Overcome

After His baptism, Jesus, following the guidance of the Holy Spirit, was led into the wilderness for forty days. Although there were wild beasts, the angels of God ministered to Him and protected Him. But Satan, knowing the power of the anointing of the Spirit, immediately began to tempt and test Jesus.

This is a template of what happens in the lives of Christians today. When the anointing of the Holy Spirit comes upon you, there may be physical attacks (wild beasts) and spiritual attacks (the devil), but if you are led by the Spirit, angels will minister to you and you will be protected.

> **Are they not all ministering spirits sent forth to minister for those who will inherit salvation?**
>
> **Hebrews 1:14**

> **Behold, I give you the authority to trample on serpents and scorpions, and over all the power of the enemy, and nothing shall by any means hurt you.**
>
> **Luke 10:19**

Although Jesus was led by the Holy Spirit into the wilderness, physical and spiritual protection was provided by the Holy Spirit. As with Daniel in the lion's den, the beasts were subdued.

The Spirit Upon Him

After leaving the wilderness and after learning that John had been put into prison, Jesus departed to Galilee. Then He went to Nazareth where He had been raised, and as His custom was, He went to the synagogue on the Sabbath and stood up to read.

When they handed Him the book of the prophet Isaiah, He opened the book and He read: *"The Spirit of the Lord is upon Me, because He has anointed Me to preach the gospel to the poor; He has sent Me to heal the brokenhearted, to proclaim liberty to the captives and recovery of sight to the blind, to set at liberty those who are oppressed; to proclaim the acceptable year of the Lord"* (Luke 4:18-19). Then He closed the book, gave it back to the attendant and sat down. He told them, *"Today this Scripture is fulfilled in your hearing"* (Luke 4:21).

Needless to say, this caused quite a stir in the synagogue, and they even attempted to kill Him. But the point is this. Jesus defined the anointing of the Holy Spirit. He said because the Holy Spirit had anointed Him, He was commissioned to do the following things: 1) to preach the gospel to the poor, 2) to heal the brokenhearted, 3) to proclaim liberty to the captives, 4) to heal the blind, 5) to release people who are oppressed, and 6) to proclaim the acceptable year of the Lord.

When the Holy Spirit is present, His anointing seeks to accomplish the same purpose. We cannot limit the Holy Spirit to one gift, an emotion, or manifestation, but must allow Him to work to the fullness of His purpose in our lives.

God anointed Jesus of Nazareth with the Holy Spirit and with power, who went about doing good and healing all who were oppressed by the devil, for God was with Him.

Acts 10:38

What is the Anointing?

The word *Christ* comes from the Greek word *Christos,* which means Messiah or Anointed One. Christ is not the last name of Jesus, but rather His transliterated designation. Translated properly, Jesus Christ means Jesus the Messiah, or Jesus the Anointed One. He was anointed with the Holy Spirit and power and we can walk in that same anointing when we receive the Holy Spirit.

The literal translation of *anointing* means to pour oil and rub it in, as was the process when kings of Israel were ceremonially proclaimed as king. We understand the anointing oil was a type and shadow of the Holy Spirit that was yet to come, but in New Testament times anointing means so much more.

In the New Testament, elders in the church are instructed to anoint the sick with oil for healing (James 5:14). The oil is representative of the Holy Spirit and we must remember oil is not the source of healing; it is the Holy Spirit who heals. The oil is only a symbol of what the Holy Spirit does.

The anointing is the applying or the transfer of the power of God by the Holy Spirit that is placed upon a person to do a specific task that the Spirit of God wants accomplished. When Jesus said that the Holy Spirit was upon Him, He said the Holy Spirit had anointed Him for a purpose. In other words, the Spirit of God empowered Him with everything needed to accomplish the task He had been given.

When a Christian is called of God to be a pastor, a teacher, an evangelist, etc., the Holy Spirit anoints or empowers the person who is called with every ability needed to accomplish their calling. We could say they were anointed for the task. Another way of looking at it is this. Because we receive power when the Holy Spirit has come upon us to do the work of the ministry, the Holy Spirit Himself is the anointing of God imparted to man for the work of ministry.

> **You have an anointing from the Holy One, and you know all things. The anointing which you have received from Him abides in you, and you do not need that anyone teach you; but as the same anointing teaches you concerning all things, and is true, and is not a lie, and just as it has taught you, you will abide in Him.**
>
> **1 John 2:20,27**

In John 14, Jesus said He was going to be with the Father and when He left, the Father would send the Holy Spirit in His name to be here with us as our Comforter and Helper until He, Jesus, returns.

Jesus Prophesies the Coming of the Spirit

Shortly before the arrest of Jesus that led to His crucifixion, He spent time with His disciples and instructed them concerning things that were to come. He told them if they loved Him, they would keep His commandments. He also said He would ask the Father to give His disciples another Advocate who would assist them and be with them forever. He called this Advocate the Spirit of truth.

But the Advocate, the Holy Spirit, whom the Father will send in my name, will teach you all things and will remind you of everything I have said to you.

John 14:26 (NIV)

When the Advocate comes, whom I will send to you from the Father — the Spirit of truth who goes out from the Father — He will testify about me.

John 15:26 (NIV)

He went on to tell them the world would not accept the Spirit of truth because the world doesn't know Him. Then He told His disciples they knew the Spirit of truth because He was with them, and in the future not only would He be with them, but He would be in them.

The Spirit of truth, whom the world cannot receive, because it neither sees Him nor knows Him; but you know Him, for He dwells with you and will be in you.

John 14:17

Although at this time the disciples did not understand what He was saying, He was actually foretelling that the Holy Spirit would inhabit born-again believers after the church was established. He continued by telling them it would not be long before He would no longer be seen on the earth by the world, but that His followers would live because He would also live. He said, *"On that day you will realize that I am in My Father, and you are in Me, and I am in you"* (John 14:20 NIV).

He told them the Father would send the Holy Spirit, and not only would He teach them all things, but He would remind them of everything He had spoken to them. A while later He told His disciples it was necessary for Him to leave because the Advocate, the Holy Spirit, would not come to them unless He (Jesus) left (John 16:7).

Jesus revealed insight to us about the work of the Holy Spirit. He said when the Holy Spirit came, He would prove the world to be wrong about sin, righteousness, and judgment because the prince of this world would stand condemned. He told His disciples there was much more that He could say, but they could not bear it at that time (John 16:12). This implied there would be further revelation concerning the Holy Spirit that would come later.

Then He further comforted His disciples by telling them that when the Spirit of truth came, He would guide them in all truth. He would not be speaking on His own but He would tell them what was yet to come. (John 16:13.) He said the Holy Spirit would glorify Him because the Spirit is from Him. Then He made a bold statement by saying, *"All that belongs to the Father is mine. That is why I said the Spirit will receive from me what he will make known to you"* (John 16:15 NIV).

Jesus clearly told His disciples that He was leaving, but He would not leave them like orphans (John 14:18). He told them the Holy Spirit would not only be with them, but very soon would be in them and show them things to come.

But very truly I tell you, it is for your good that I am going away. Unless I go away, the Advocate will not come to you; but if I go, I will send him to you.

John 16:7 (NIV)

I have much more to say to you, more than you can now bear. But when he, the Spirit of truth, comes, he will guide you into all the truth. He will not speak on his own; he will speak only what he hears, and he will tell you what is yet to come.

John 16:12-13 (NIV)

CHAPTER 4

THE BEGINNING OF THE CHURCH

But you shall receive power when the Holy Spirit has come upon you; and you shall be witnesses to Me in Jerusalem, and in all Judea and Samaria, and to the end of the earth."

Acts 1:8

A question I am often asked is—when did the church begin? What was the first day that the church existed? While this question may seem simplistic, it is another foundational truth that must be understood in order to understand the dimensional transfer from the law to grace. There is a marker in the timeline of man that points to a day that is the most important day in humanity. There is a day where an event took place that changed the course of history and the destiny of man. That day was the day Jesus placed His blood on the altar in heaven and completed the work of the New Covenant.

On the day of His resurrection, the stone was rolled away so that Jesus could exit the tomb. He was in His resurrected earthly physical body; however, He had not yet been glorified. When Mary Magdalene (Mark 16:9) saw Jesus after His resurrection, she was instructed not to touch Him and He explained why. *"'Don't touch me,' he cautioned, 'for I haven't yet ascended to the Father'"* (John 20:17 TLB).

But later that day when He appeared to some of the disciples, He told them to handle Him and see that He was flesh and bone (Luke 24:39). Obviously, He had ascended into heaven, placed His blood on the altar, and returned with His glorified body that could appear at the speed of thought and move without regard to earthly physics (Hebrews 9:12).

The Birth of the Church

At the very moment He placed His blood on the altar in heaven, the New Covenant began, the church existed, and Jesus took His place as the head of the church (Colossians 1:18). Having deposited His perfect blood on the altar, He returned to earth and from that point on, everyone who believed in their heart that He was the Son of God and that God raised Him from the dead, and who openly confessed this truth, was saved (Romans 10:9). They became a part of this new entity called the church. They were no longer a Jew or a Gentile, but one in Christ (Galatians 3:28).

When these new believers believed in their heart and made the confession of faith that saved them, the Holy Spirit moved inside of their spirit and they were sealed by the Holy Spirit until the day of redemption (Ephesians 4:30).

As Jesus appeared to the disciples and they shared the good news, the word spread that Jesus had been raised from the dead, and the church grew in number. For forty days Jesus taught His followers about the kingdom of God (v.3). On the fortieth day He assembled them together on the Mount of Olives.

I have been at the Mount of Olives several times and it is just a short walk across the Kidron Valley to Old Jerusalem. It was there on the Mount of Olives that He commanded His disciples to remain in Jerusalem and to wait for the Promise of the Father which, He said, "you have heard from Me" (v.4). Obviously, Jesus had explained to them in much greater detail what was going to happen in Jerusalem. Then He went on to say that although John baptized people with water, they would be baptized with the Holy Spirit in just a few days.

His disciples then asked Him when He was going to restore the kingdom to Israel. Although the restoration of Israel is important and much of the Bible is given to the end time prophecies concerning the nation of Israel, Jesus sidestepped that question by telling them that it wasn't for them to know the times or the seasons. Then He refocused them onto the subject of the Holy Spirit and said they would receive power when the Holy Spirit had come upon them. When He spoke these words, and while they watched, He started ascending into the sky until He eventually went into a cloud and they couldn't see Him any longer. (Acts 1:3-9.)

Final Instruction Before Leaving Earth

My children are adults, but when they were younger and living at home, there would be times that I needed to leave them alone at the house for a while. As I was leaving, I usually gave them instructions, but the final instructions I gave them were always the most important. After reviewing what they could do and what they couldn't do, my final instruction would be the thing that I felt was most important for them to not forget.

Likewise, there were forty days of instructions given to the disciples and I'm sure that many subjects were discussed. But when it came time for Jesus to ascend and leave these young Christians alone, He focused and refocused their attention to the Holy Spirit. He ascended and took His place seated at the right hand of the Father and these who had believed in their heart and confessed with their mouth that He was Lord, waited in Jerusalem for the Promise.

The Promise was a Gift. The Promise was a Counselor. The Promise was a Helper. The Promise they were waiting for was the Holy Spirit.

The Day the Holy Spirit Came

After returning to Jerusalem, they went into the upper room where they were staying. Approximately 120 people, which included His disciples, His brothers, His mother Mary, and several other women, were gathered there where they continued in prayer. (Acts 1:12-15.)

The next week, when the Day of Pentecost arrived and while they were seated in the upper room praying with unity of spirit, a sound came from heaven. This sound was so strong that it sounded like a rushing mighty wind. This sound filled the entire house where they were sitting. (Acts 2:1-2.)

It's interesting to note that at this time in history, there were no electronic sound systems, there were no jet engines, there were no trains, there were no atomic bombs. The greatest noise of the day that could be described was the wind of a storm. This was how the writer described what they heard when the noise from heaven entered the room. Immediately, divided tongues that looked like fire sat on each of them and they were all filled with the Holy Spirit and began to speak with other tongues as the Holy Spirit gave them utterance. (Acts 2:3-4.)

Many have taught that this was the birth of the church. While I understand the generality of the statement, we must remember that the church was birthed at the moment the sacrifice, the blood of Jesus, was placed on the altar in heaven. From that point, everyone who believed in their heart and confessed with their mouth that Jesus Christ was Lord was born again. The church grew as people believed in Him and confessed their belief. This early church was instructed by Jesus Himself for forty days. They spent the time remaining until the Day of Pentecost together praying in unity in the upper room.

The Day of Pentecost was not the day they became Christians, but it was the day that the 120 who were Christians had a second experience. It was the day they were filled with the Holy Spirit to overflowing and spoke in tongues.

When a person believes in their heart that Jesus Christ is the Son of God, they are saved and the Holy Spirit moves inside of their spirit and they experience eternal life (John 20:22).

However, there is a second experience that takes place after a person is born again. It could be moments or it could be years, but either way, it is a second experience. It is the filling of the Holy Spirit and power that is manifested with a lifestyle of walking in the fruit of the Spirit and yielding to the gifts of the Spirit.

The Upper Room Outpouring

During the time of Jesus, Pentecost was an annual Jewish festival, also known as the "Feast of Weeks," or the "Day of Firstfruits," a celebration of the first buds of the harvest. Jewish men were required by law to go to Jerusalem three times each year to celebrate the major feasts and Pentecost was one of them. It took place seven weeks and a day after Passover.

During this time, there were devoted men from every nation in Jerusalem. When the sound occurred in the upper room, it was so great that it drew thousands of people together. Those in Jerusalem were greatly confused because they all heard the new Christians speaking in their own native language. They were astonished because the ones speaking in their language were Galileans, and Galileans were known for their lack of education. (Acts 2:5-8.)

There were Parthians, Medes, Elamites, and people who lived in Mesopotamia, Judea, Cappadocia, Pontus, Asia, Phrygia, Pamphylia, Egypt, Libya, Cyrene, Rome, Cretans, and Arabs and they were all saying the same thing. "We hear these Galileans speaking in our own native language the wonderful works of God." Again, they were amazed and perplexed saying to each other "Whatever could this mean?" And, of course, there were others who mocked and said they were just drunk. (Acts 2:9-13.)

Peter's Sermon

Up until the Day of Pentecost, Peter had not been one of the strong outspoken disciples. In fact, quite the opposite. When Jesus was being accused after His arrest, Peter was recognized and asked if he was an associate of Jesus. Three times he denied knowing the Lord. Putting it bluntly, he was a timid coward, too afraid to stand up for his Friend.

But on the Day of Pentecost, Peter was a different man. He boldly stood up in front of the multitude, along with the other eleven disciples. By this time Judas had been replaced with Matthias (Acts 1:26). Peter wasn't timid or afraid, but stood boldly and preached to the men of Israel. He quoted from the book of Joel and he quoted King David and eloquently stated his case to the multitude.

He told them the Promise was to them, to their children, and to all who were afar off and as many as our God would call (Acts 2:39). He continued speaking, testifying, and exhorting them, encouraging them to be saved from this perverse generation.

About 3,000 people received the word he spoke and were baptized that very day. The church continued in fellowship and they steadfastly walked in the teachings of the apostles. As they continued daily in unity in the temple, they broke bread with each other from house to house while praising God. They had favor with all the people and the Lord added to the church daily those who were being saved. (Acts 2:40-47.)

The Healings Begin

In these early days of the Spirit-filled church, Peter and John went to the temple during the time of prayer, and there they encountered a man who had been crippled from birth. Every day this man was carried to the gate of the temple and he laid there asking for alms. On this particular day, as Peter and John walked past him as they prepared to enter the temple, the man reached out and asked for alms.

During this time of Jewish history, begging at the temple gate was not something anyone could do just because they wanted to. There was a process of certification that people in need had to pass before they were allowed to beg. In fact, there was a certain garment or coat that signified they had been certified. This process kept those who would pretend to be in need from collecting alms that should go to those who were truly needy. This lets us know that the man at the temple gate begging for money was truly crippled.

Peter stopped and locked eyes with the beggar and said, "Look at us." The beggar thought he was going to receive what he was asking for. He was asking for money. But under the anointing of the Holy Spirit, Peter gave him more than he was asking for. He said, *"Silver and gold I do not have. But what I do have I give to you: In the name of Jesus Christ of Nazareth, rise up and walk"* (v.6). Then Peter reached out, took the beggar by the right hand and pulled him up. Immediately the feet and ankles of the beggar received strength, and not only did he stand up and walk, but he started leaping and praising God.

When he entered the temple with Peter and John, the excitement of his healing was overwhelming. As he continued walking and praising God, the eyes of all the people were upon him because they knew he was the one who had been begging at the gate called Beautiful at the entrance of the temple.

As Peter and John stood at the temple, the lame man who had just been healed was clinging to Peter and John and the crowd ran toward them in amazement. When Peter saw what was happening, he took this second opportunity to proclaim the good news of Jesus. He said, *"Men of Israel, why do you marvel at this? Or why look so intently at us as though by our own power or godliness we made this man walk?"* (v.12). Then proclaiming many truths to them, he told them the faith which comes through Jesus (the Word of God) is what gave this man his healing. (Acts 3:1-16.)

> When they (the Sanhedrin) had placed them in the center, they began to inquire, "By what power, or in what name, have you done this?" Then Peter, filled with the Holy Spirit, said to them, "Rulers and elders of the people...let it be known to all of you and to all the people of Israel, that by the name of Jesus Christ the Nazarene..., this man stands here before you in good health..."

Now as they observed the confidence of Peter and John and understood that they were uneducated and untrained men, they were amazed, and began to recognize them as having been with Jesus.

Acts 4:7,8,10,13 NASB

Filled with the Power

This healing was just one of the many manifestations that was to occur as a result of Peter and John being filled with the Holy Spirit in the upper room. It is interesting to note that from the day the church began on the day of the resurrection until the upper room experience, no healings or miraculous events were recorded at the hands of these new church members. But once they were filled with the Holy Spirit, a change in the miraculous power manifested in their lives took place.

In the same way that no miracles were recorded at the hands of Jesus until the Holy Spirit came upon Him in the Jordan River, no miracles were recorded in the new creation called the church until the church received the baptism of the Holy Spirit.

CHAPTER 5

THE HOLY SPIRIT AND THE CHURCH

He who has an ear, let him hear what the Spirit says
to the churches.

Revelation 3:6

Some denominational churches ignore or teach very little about the Holy Spirit. Others distort the teaching and the administration of the Holy Spirit to reflect the denominational or associational teachings that their church is subject to. For a pastor or a church to ignore teaching about the Holy Spirit and yielding to Him is to deprive their congregation of the power that Jesus said would come upon them.

Throughout my many years of ministry, I have encountered many teachings concerning the Holy Spirit that were strange or unbalanced. In fact, I have sat in meetings and listened to well-meaning teachers teach exactly the opposite of what the Word of God teaches. While these teachers may have good intentions and desire to help people, once again, they are depriving their followers of the miraculous power to change lives that only comes through the gifts of the Holy Spirit.

In First Timothy 4, Paul prophesied concerning the end of days. He said that during this time there would be teachers who would follow after their own lusts and there would be others who would actually teach doctrines of demons.

Now the Spirit expressly says that in latter times some will depart from the faith, giving heed to deceiving spirits and doctrines of demons.

1 Timothy 4:1

The word *doctrine* comes from the Greek word *didaché* which simply means teaching. With this in mind, we must ask ourselves this question. What is it that demons would teach? Of course, they would not teach anything that would assist or help a Christian in their life. Jesus said the enemy comes to steal, kill, and destroy (John 10:10). That is the mission statement of the devil. So, it is easy to determine that the demonic spirits under his command would teach things that are destructive and deadly.

Many Christians suffer defeat and devastation in life and some even are subject to early death because the teaching they follow is not from the Lord, but rather deceptive teaching that originates with demons. Deception, by its very nature, takes something that is false and makes it appear to be true. Deception can make darkness appear to be light, and death appear to be life. When deception is followed to the end of its course, it brings destruction.

But know this, that in the last days perilous times will come: For men will be lovers of themselves,

lovers of money, boasters, proud, blasphemers, dis-
obedient to parents, unthankful, unholy, unloving,
unforgiving, slanderers, without self-control, brutal,
despisers of good, traitors, headstrong, haughty, lovers of pleasure rather than lovers of God, having a
form of godliness but denying its power. And from
such people turn away! ... always learning and never
able to come to the knowledge of the truth.

2 Timothy 3:1-5,7

The Judgment Seat of Christ

Paul said there would be a day when he and every Christian
would stand before Jesus and give an account for what we
have done, whether it be good or whether it be bad.

For we must all appear before the judgment seat of
Christ, that each one may receive the things done
in the body, according to what he has done, whether
good or bad.

2 Corinthians 5:10

As a Christian, when you stand before Jesus at the judgment seat of Christ, your salvation will not be judged. Your
salvation was completed when you accepted Jesus as your
Lord and Savior. While your eternal life is not being judged,
because you already have it, your works will be judged. And
the point is this. You will be judged on what you have done,
not what you intended to do. Even though your intentions
may be good in life, if you submit to false teaching and follow

it, there is no reward. Deception will make a person believe they are believing right and doing right, when they are actually believing and doing wrong.

Correcting Deceptive Teaching

For many years of my life, I believed that the gifts of the Holy Spirit passed away when the last apostle of the New Testament died. Why did I believe this? It's because that is what I was taught. The only problem was, when I looked for verification of that teaching in the Word of God, I could not find it. Why? Because the Word of God teaches exactly the opposite. The gifts of the Holy Spirit were given to the church at the beginning of the church age (or the last days), and will continue in the church until Jesus comes and appears in the sky and the church is taken away to the judgment seat of Christ and the marriage supper of the Lamb in heaven.

The Bible clearly gives the church instruction on how to walk in the Spirit, pray in the Spirit, and receive the gifts of the Spirit. If the moving of the Holy Spirit was only for the first century church, then the instructions given to us through the Holy Scriptures would be irrelevant and none of the Word of God is irrelevant.

> **All Scripture is given by inspiration of God, and is profitable for doctrine, for reproof, for correction, for instruction in righteousness.**
>
> **2 Timothy 3:16**

If the gifts of the Holy Spirit were only for the church at Corinth, Paul would have said so and probably would have told them verbally instead of writing it down.

Prophecy is being fulfilled at an accelerated rate. The rebirth of the nation of Israel and the rise of the nations of prophecy as listed in the Bible all let us know that the return of Jesus, the Messiah, is near. Biblical prophecy also tells us as we near the end of man's days on the earth, the world will become worse. We are seeing all these things happen. (2 Timothy 3:1,12-13.)

As Christians in these last days, we must take advantage of the power that Jesus prophesied would come upon the church when we receive the Holy Spirit (Acts 1:8).

The Holy Spirit is God. God is light and light always overpowers darkness. As children of light we are the carriers of the gospel and the power. If we walk in the fulness of the strength and power of the anointing, then nothing shall by any means hurt us (Luke 10:19), and we will fulfill the great commission (Matthew 28:19) by letting our light shine.

> **Let your light so shine before men, that they may see your good works and glorify your Father in heaven.**
>
> **Matthew 5:16**

The Gospel of Power

For our gospel did not come to you in word only, but also in power, and in the Holy Spirit and in much

assurance, as you know what kind of men we were among you for your sake.

1 Thessalonians 1:5

The world is entertained with movies, games, and sporting events, but movies, games, and sporting events will never transform an alcoholic, will never heal the crippled, or restore a broken life to fullness. Only the revelation of the Word through the demonstration of power by the Holy Spirit will accomplish this.

One of the greatest deceptions of the modern church is the idea that to attract the world, we must show the world that we understand them by looking like and acting like them. The tolerance of sin through the searing of the conscience (1 Timothy 4:1-2) dulls the message of the gospel and eliminates the need for repentance. Of course, we do not want to be condemning and judgmental, but we cannot accept or ignore sin in order to draw the world to the church.

The Holy Spirit does not condemn man (John 3:17). Man has already done that to himself (John 3:18). But the power of the Holy Spirit through the manifestations of the gifts of the Spirit and the lifestyle of the fruit of the Spirit will shed light into the dark places and expose the sin. Then once the sin is exposed, without condemnation but through love, the choice can be made to repent and turn away from the darkness of the world.

I have seen Christians spend hours trying to intellectually explain to a nonbeliever why they must repent. While it is good to share the Scriptures, we must never forget that the revelation of the Scriptures only comes through the work of the Holy Spirit. Remember, Paul said that spiritual things could not be understood by the natural mind (1 Corinthians 2:14). This is why Paul did not approach people only through natural persuasive words of wisdom, but by the power and demonstration of the Holy Spirit (1 Corinthians 2:4).

Unclean Spirits

Several times in the Bible, Jesus spoke to demonic spirits and they left. He gave instruction about what takes place when a demonic spirit leaves a person. Jesus said when an unclean spirit goes out of a person, it passes through waterless places seeking rest.

Jesus went on to say when these unclean spirits do not find any rest, in desperation they return to the body they left. If that body is swept clean and has not been filled with the Spirit of God, the evil spirit re-enters with seven other spirits who are more evil. The result is the man who was delivered is in seven times worse condition than before his deliverance. (Luke 11:24-26.)

Not only do we learn from this passage that there are varying degrees of evil among the demonic spirits, but we also learn there is a responsibility to fill the emptiness within a lost person who has been delivered from demonic oppression with the Holy Spirit. Deliverance without salvation accomplishes nothing. In fact, it creates a worse situation for the person who has been delivered.

Playing with Fire

For two years Paul lived in Asia and preached the Word of the Lord Jesus to both the Jews and the Gentiles. During this time, God worked many unusual miracles through him. There were times when handkerchiefs or aprons that had touched his body were taken to people who were sick and the diseases left them. It's also interesting to note that the anointing on the handkerchiefs and aprons even caused evil spirits to leave those who were possessed. (Acts 19:11-12.)

As his fame grew and people saw the results of these unusual miracles, they attempted to imitate his actions and duplicate the miracles they had observed. Sceva, a Jewish priest, had seven sons who attempted to duplicate Paul's miracles. They spoke to a demon-possessed man by saying, "We exorcise you by the Jesus whom Paul preaches." The evil spirit answered and said, "Jesus I know, and Paul I know; but who are you?" Immediately the man who was possessed of the evil spirit overpowered them, beat them, and stripped them of their clothing and they fled naked. (Acts 19:13-16.)

This event that occurred during the early years of the church explains another spiritual truth concerning the spirit world. Attempting to operate in the things of the spirit without the anointing of the Holy Spirit is dangerous. Even though these young Jewish men had been raised in the family of a Jewish priest, they were not born again, they did not have the Holy Spirit living inside of them, and had not been given the authority over the power of the enemy. The result was that they fled stripped and whipped. As a Christian, you should always be led by the Holy Spirit when encountering the forces of the enemy.

Entertainment and Showmanship

Many years ago during the charismatic move that swept across this nation and the world, there was a great man of God who, under the anointing of the Holy Spirit during one of his meetings, stepped forward and simply blew onto the crowd. Many people were healed and delivered in that meeting. But as word traveled as to what had happened, ministers everywhere started blowing on their congregations.

Never take action in the realm of the spirit in order to imitate the actions of someone else. While it is true that Paul said to imitate him as he imitates Christ (1 Corinthians 11:1), he was referring to his character and walk with the Lord, not to specific gifts of the Spirit. Imitation is good when it comes to things of character and holiness, but when moving under the anointing of the Holy Spirit, you must be led by the Holy Spirit. Entertainment and showmanship will never duplicate the supernatural, miraculous power of the Holy Spirit.

Is the Promise for the Church Today?

Earlier in the book, we discussed the Day of Pentecost and how the early Christians who had only been saved for a matter of weeks received the Holy Spirit. But let's look at this story again from a different perspective. Is the promise of the Holy Spirit and speaking in tongues for the church today? Was the promise for that generation only or was it for their descendants?

On the Day of Pentecost, after the Holy Spirit had filled the disciples in the upper room and the multitudes had heard them speaking in their own native language, Peter stood up with the other eleven disciples and raised his voice and began to explain what had happened that day. He told the multitude that it was the fulfillment of a prophecy that was spoken by the prophet, Joel. He told them about Jesus and how He was crucified. He told them that God raised Jesus from the dead.

When he concluded his sermon, he made a very important statement. Peter said, *"Repent, and let every one of you be baptized in the name of Jesus Christ for the remission of sins; and you shall receive the gift of the Holy Spirit"* (Acts 2:38).

Then Peter went on to say that the gift of the Holy Spirit was not just for the one hundred and twenty in the upper room or for the multitude listening, but the gift of the Holy Spirit was also for their children and the generations to come. In other words, receiving the Holy Spirit is for everyone who desires to receive Him. That includes you and me.

For the promise is to you and to your children, and to all who are afar off, as many as the Lord our God will call.

Acts 2:39

CHAPTER 6

THE SECOND EXPERIENCE

> When they had come down, [they] prayed for them
> that they might receive the Holy Spirit. For as yet He
> had fallen upon none of them. They had only been
> baptized in the name of the Lord Jesus. Then they laid
> hands on them, and they received the Holy Spirit.
>
> **Acts 8:15-17**

When a person becomes a Christian, the Holy Spirit moves inside of them to live permanently, for all eternity (John 14:16). When this happens, there are several terms that apply. Some say the person is saved, born again, became a Christian, or received Christ as their Lord and Savior. All of these terms are correct and simply refer to the moment when a person surrenders their life to God. This is when the Scripture says old things pass away, all things become new, and this person is now a new creation (2 Corinthians 5:17). No longer are they considered a Jew or a Gentile, but now are rather a born-again Christian and a part of the church and body of Jesus Christ (Galatians 3:28).

Although this miraculous life-changing event is the greatest gift from God available to mankind, it is not His final gift. There is a second gift called the baptism of the Holy Spirit, or receiving the Holy Spirit, and what I like to refer to as the second experience.

Let's take a look at what the Bible says about this second experience.

The Gospel in Samaria

Before Saul had his encounter with Jesus on the road to Damascus, he was a leader in the persecution of the church which was at Jerusalem. Because of this great persecution, Christians were scattered throughout the regions of Judea and Samaria, except for the apostles who remained in Jerusalem. It was during this time that Stephen was martyred and Saul was doing everything within his power to destroy the church (Acts 7:58-59). He had the authority to enter houses and arrest men and women and throw them into prison just because they believed Jesus was the Messiah.

As so often happens during times of great persecution, the Christians who were scattered intensified in their belief and the church continued to grow. As a result of the scattering of Christians, Philip went down to the city of Samaria and preached the gospel to them. As the multitudes of people heard and responded to the truths spoken by Philip, they accepted his teaching and experienced the manifestation of many miracles. Also, demonic spirits were cast out of many people who were possessed and others who were paralyzed or crippled were healed. Of course, the result of all of this was great joy throughout the city.

Also living in the city of Samaria was a sorcerer named Simon. For a long time he had astonished the people of Samaria and claimed that he was someone great. Before the arrival of Philip, the people of Samaria had called this man "the great power of God" (v. 10) because he had astonished them with his magic for many years.

However, when the people of Samaria believed everything Philip preached concerning the kingdom of God and the name of Jesus Christ, they made a public confession by being baptized. In fact, Simon the sorcerer also believed and was baptized. After his baptism, he followed Philip and was amazed when he saw the true miracles and true signs that were done. (Acts 8:1-13.)

Let's review what happened in Samaria:

1. Philip preached Christ to them.
2. They all heard and received the things spoken by Philip.
3. Miracles were manifest.
4. Demonic spirits came out of the ones who were possessed.
5. Paralyzed and crippled people were healed.
6. They had great joy.
7. They believed the things Philip preached concerning the kingdom of God and the name of Jesus Christ.
8. They were baptized.

9. Even the opposition (sorcerer) believed and was baptized.

By every biblical standard, the people of Samaria were Christians. If the events that took place there were to take place today, no one would doubt that the people had experienced true salvation, because they believed in and confessed the name of Jesus Christ. They openly proclaimed this belief through baptism by a man of God who had been preaching the Word.

The Apostles in Jerusalem Heard the Good News

Remember, during this time in history there were no daily newspapers, postal service, telephones, or Internet. News traveled slowly from person to person, by word of mouth, or by writings. Texting and email did not exist, so even the writing of letters was a slow process. When the news of what happened in Samaria reached the apostles in Jerusalem, they were pleased to hear that Samaria had received the Word of God. This is another confirmation the people of Samaria were Christians.

> Now when the apostles who were at Jerusalem heard that Samaria had received the word of God, they sent Peter and John to them.
>
> Acts 8:14

However, the apostles decided to send Peter and John to Samaria. After their travel from Jerusalem, they prayed for the people of Samaria to receive the Holy Spirit, for as yet He had fallen upon none of them (Acts 8:16). According to the apostles, the people of Samaria had only been baptized in the name of the Lord Jesus, so they laid hands on them and they received the Holy Spirit (Acts 8:17). This definitively proves that even though a person is a Christian and has the Holy Spirit living within their spirit, there is a second experience for the Christian called receiving the Holy Spirit.

It Was Noticeable

Obviously, receiving the Holy Spirit was more than the apostles simply laying hands on the people of Samaria, because Simon the magician saw something happen that was so significant through the laying on of the apostles hands, that he offered them money. In fact, he said, *"Give me this power also that anyone on whom I lay hands may receive the Holy Spirit"* (Acts 8:19).

I've heard many ministers talk about the evilness of Simon the sorcerer because he offered money and because Peter rebuked him. We must never forget Simon was a new Christian with a satanic past. Simon was like most young Christians I have met who also desire this ability when they see the power of the Holy Spirit changing lives through the laying on of hands and the miraculous manifestations that take place.

But the point I am wanting to make is this. The apostles laid hands on the people of Samaria who had already received Jesus as Lord and been baptized. Something happened that was visible to Simon that was so dramatic he asked to purchase this power the apostles possessed.

Truly, receiving the Holy Spirit is a second experience for those who have received Jesus as Lord that can either be received or quenched. Remember, as a believer we only receive what we believe.

Supernatural Miracle Power

God anointed Jesus of Nazareth with the Holy Spirit and with power, who went about doing good and healing all who were oppressed by the devil, for God was with Him.

Acts 10:38

While Peter was in Joppa talking to Cornelius, his relatives, and close friends, he made a very interesting statement. He said that God had anointed Jesus with the Holy Spirit and power and He went about doing good and healing all who were oppressed by the devil. A nugget of truth that is hidden away in this statement is this. The healing of the oppressed by Jesus took place after He was anointed by the Holy Spirit, and the power to heal was included with the anointing.

Remember, in all of the gospels there is not one miracle recorded at the hands of Jesus until <u>after</u> the Holy Spirit came upon Him in the Jordan River. But immediately after that event, He was empowered to heal the sick, raise the dead, and defy earthly physics. He later told His disciples in John 14 they would do the same works that He did, only greater (v. 12).

Remember also, just before He ascended into heaven forty-three days after His crucifixion, He told His disciples they would receive power after the Holy Spirit had come upon them (Acts 1:8). There is a direct correlation between supernatural miracle power and being filled with the Holy Spirit.

Receiving the Holy Spirit is for All Who Believe

While Peter was speaking the truths of God to the family of Cornelius and their friends, the Holy Spirit fell upon all of them who heard the Word spoken by Peter. Peter had brought with him some of his Jewish friends who were believers in Jesus. All of them were astonished because the gift of the Holy Spirit had been poured out onto Cornelius, his family, and his friends, and they heard them speak with tongues and magnify God.

Why were they so astonished? It's because Cornelius and his family, and probably all of his friends, were Gentiles. Up until this time the baptism of the Holy Spirit had only been poured out onto the Jews. Why is this? Quite simply, it's because all of the early Christians were Jews.

When it became obvious they wanted to be baptized, Peter said that baptism could not be forbidden to them because these Gentiles had received the Holy Spirit in the same way the Jews had received. So they were baptized by water.

This answers a question often asked: Must a person be baptized with water before they can receive the baptism of the Holy Spirit? By this biblical example in Acts chapter 10, we know positively that baptism by water is not required to receive the baptism of the Holy Spirit. The baptism of the

Holy Spirit is available for all who believe in Jesus Christ and receive Him as their Savior.

The Disciples of John Received the Holy Spirit

On his third missionary journey, after he passed through the upper regions, Paul passed through Ephesus and found twelve disciples of John the Baptist. He asked them a very interesting question. He asked, "Did you receive the Holy Spirit when you believed?" They responded by saying they had not even heard about the Holy Spirit or that the Holy Spirit even existed. In other words, they had no knowledge, no teaching, or no understanding about the Holy Spirit.

Then Paul asked them, "Into what then were you baptized?" And they said, "Into John's baptism." Then Paul explained to them John was baptizing people into the belief that the Messiah was coming soon and the Messiah was Christ Jesus. When they heard this, they were baptized in the name of the Lord Jesus. After their baptism, Paul laid hands on them and the Holy Spirit came upon them and they spoke with tongues and prophesied. (Acts 19:1-6.)

This is another example of New Testament believers receiving the Holy Spirit through the laying on of hands separately from the time of their salvation.

Baptist Background

My background is a Baptist background. I was raised in the home of an ordained Baptist deacon for a father, and my mother was a Baptist Sunday School teacher. I personally received Jesus Christ as my Lord and Savior while attending a Baptist Vacation Bible School at the age of seven after a Baptist minister taught our class about the horrors of hell. In fact, he preached like he had just gotten back.

As a Christian, I was baptized at the First Baptist Church in Raytown, Missouri at the age of twelve and as a teenager I played in the Baptist bell choir and we performed at the Southern Baptist Convention. It was there I felt called to be a Baptist minister. I attended a Baptist university where I met a Baptist girl studying to be a Baptist missionary. We were married in the Baptist church in Clinton, Missouri. I became the pastor of a Baptist church. It would be safe to say that I lived in a very Baptist world!

The Beginning of My Understanding

Because of my Baptist background as a child and teenager, and to fulfill my call to the ministry, my parents and I decided I should attend Southwest Baptist University (it was called Southwest Baptist College at that time).

While attending SBU, I was a member of the campus ministerial association. I was young, majoring in theology, and preaching any time I got a chance. My sermons were not very long in those days. Most churches where I spoke wanted the minister to speak between fifteen and twenty minutes. I would study and plan my sermon for days. I remember taking my notes and walking in the park, preaching my sermon to the animals that were there. Try as I might, I had trouble getting past ten minutes.

I bought a book called "Knight's Master Book of 4,000 Illustrations." This was a book full of stories and illustrations that could be used from the pulpit. The stories were divided into categories so a minister could take his subject, look it up, and come up with some witty little sayings to enhance his sermon.

I had another book that was a textbook for one of my theological classes titled, "Snappy Sermon Starters." Between these two books and the Bible, I could sometimes gather fifteen minutes of preaching—if I talked slow.

Back in those days, I was mainly speaking at rural Baptist churches that were nestled deep in the Ozarks that had trouble finding anyone to fill their pulpit. They contacted the school and the school sent me. While I was doing everything I could to make my sermons last longer, I could tell the congregation was wanting them to be shorter. There wasn't much power in my messages in those days, to say the least!

It was during this time as a freshman theology student that I met my wife, Loretta. I remember one evening after classes we were driving around in my 1963 two door Chevrolet Impala and talking about the things of God. She likewise had been raised a Baptist and was at Southwest Baptist University studying to be a missionary. While driving along, as with most young people, our conversation leaned toward us asking questions about each other. I said, "Tell me a little about yourself spiritually." She paused and said, "I haven't spoken at any meetings or traveled for the gospel, but I have been filled with the Holy Spirit and I speak in tongues."

I will never forget the panic I felt at that moment. I remember grabbing the steering wheel with both hands so I wouldn't veer off into the ditch. What was I going to do?!? My girlfriend was one of "those people!" I don't remember much of what happened the rest of the evening; but I do remember being back at the dorm that night in Memorial Hall, room 324, and recalling what had taken place when my grandmother (on my father's side) had taken me to her Pentecostal church.

I was a young child and my grandmother didn't drive, so we walked down the gravel road from her house in Climax Springs, Missouri to the little Pentecostal church. When we walked into the sanctuary, everything seemed normal. I remember people smiling, being nice, and several musicians heading toward the platform. That in itself was a little different for me, because the Baptist church I attended with my parents had a piano and an organ and a choir. So seeing several people grab guitars and head toward the platform was a little unusual.

As the minister walked to the platform and took the microphone, everything seemed normal until he said, "Let us pray." Everybody in the auditorium started praying—loudly. Hands went up in the air. Some people started shouting. The guitars started playing, and there was a mixture of loud country gospel music and shouting. People started walking around and bouncing off the walls, falling on their knees, lying on the floor, and it scared me! I remember dropping to my knees and trying to get under the pew. To me it was sheer pandemonium.

Even though I was just a child, I thought those people were crazy and anyone who acted like that had mental problems or was unstable. Years later, I remember thinking it must have been mass hypnosis.

So, when my future wife told me she spoke in tongues, I quit taking her to church. I envisioned the minister reading from the Bible and coming across the words "Holy Spirit" and something would snap inside of her, she would roll on the floor, swing from the chandelier, and start speaking in tongues. Then I envisioned being called into the administration office at the university, being relieved of my Baptist credentials and being asked to leave.

Years later, the Lord spoke to me during a time of prayer and said, "Sometimes people act in faith and it looks crazy to the world. But there are those who act crazy and call it faith." I'm sure the people at my grandmother's church were good people, and very possibly, because I was a young child, I was shocked and afraid because I didn't understand.

However, this event in my life has made me realize the proof that the manifestation of the Spirit is present has nothing to do with how loudly we shout, how vigorously we dance, or the music we play. But it is by the deliverance, repentance, and comfort that is brought through His presence.

Biscuits and Gravy

All through the early years of my life and ministry, I always felt like something was missing. No matter how much I would study the Word to prepare a lesson, no matter how many church services I attended or preached, it seemed as though I was not complete.

It was during this time of searching that I was asked to be the president of the men's brotherhood fellowship at a local Baptist church. This church had a large congregation for a small rural town and the men's group was very active. We met on Saturdays and it was the duty of the president to organize a testimony and a Scripture reading. For many decades, the tradition had been that the president would make the gravy that was served at the breakfast. These men loved to eat! Most of them, being farmers, were accustomed to a large country breakfast consisting of sausage, eggs, toast, coffee, biscuits and gravy.

I remember practicing and learning how to make the gravy. I had never been much of a cook growing up. Like most young men of the sixties, I was more interested in the Beatles and lava lamps. But being in this rural community, I did my best to fit in and bring to the men of the church a spiritual experience at the Saturday morning fellowship. My goal was to dig deeper into the Word and discover what it was I was missing. Even though I knew the Word and had a major in theology, there was still a hunger that had not been satisfied.

On one particular Saturday morning, I had been praying all the way to the church, "Lord, if there is something more, if there is something deeper, if there is something more spiritual, show me." Upon arriving at the church, we had our typical Saturday morning meeting. We fixed breakfast and as the president, I made the gravy. We had our usual testimony and devotion, and then dismissed.

I had taught the devotional that day and even though I personally didn't receive much from it, I was hoping and praying the men in attendance did. As we cleaned up the meeting room and I went outside to my car, I noticed three of the older men who had attended the breakfast were standing on the sidewalk talking. There is a way of knowing or sensing when people are talking about you and I had that feeling. As they saw me standing there, they slowly walked over to me, and as they were walking, I anticipated what they were going to say.

What I wanted to hear was that they had seen a great anointing upon me that day and I was hoping that possibly they would have a testimony about how my teaching had changed their lives.

When they approached, one of the men fixed a gaze on me and with a very serious look he began to speak. He said, "This church has been here a long time and I have attended the men's fellowship meetings all of my life. In fact, Brother Wilcox has gone here all of his life and his daddy before him and we've come to this conclusion. Of all of the brotherhood presidents we have ever had in all the years that we can remember, you make the best gravy of any of them!"

I tried to smile, but my heart sank! I barely remember getting into the car. I don't recommend this to anyone, but I threw my Bible across the car. If the window on the passenger side had been down, the Bible would have ended up on the sidewalk. I said, "God, if this is all there is to being a Christian—just getting saved and baptized and hanging on for the rest of your life trying to be good, then just take me home! If this is all there is, I'm done!"

The Answer to Emptiness

Obviously, I was distraught and that was one of the low points in my spiritual life. But looking back on that day, I can understand the frustration in people's hearts. When a Christian tells me they feel spiritually empty, I now have the answer. They must be filled with the Holy Spirit. Programs, church activities, social life, or the work of the ministry by itself will never fill the void that only the Holy Spirit can fill.

The people of Samaria experienced salvation, deliverance, and great joy, but they didn't know that there was a greater power available. The apostles in Jerusalem knew it and through the laying on of hands, they imparted an additional power that was so visible that Simon the sorcerer offered to buy it.

It is possible to live your life as a Christian and never experience the baptism of the Holy Spirit. It could be because you've never been told about the Holy Spirit. Or it could be because you have been told and rejected the idea. Either way, the absence of the baptism of the Holy Spirit leaves an emptiness and a lack of fulfillment. Eternal life is wonderful, but eternal life with the Promise is better.

My Second Experience

Southwest Baptist University was considered a premier school for secular and theological studies. Because I felt the call of ministry in my heart, I enrolled in as many theology courses as I possibly could. Mathematics and biology courses were also required, but my major was theology. It was at SBU that I was going to meet a professor who would change my life forever.

As a freshman, one of my first theology class requirements was New Testament Greek. I looked forward to studying Greek because I've always enjoyed languages. In high school, I took one year of Latin and even enrolled in advanced English studies during a summer term, so I was excited to take New Testament Greek. The Greek professor was Dr. Jerry Horner, who was the Chairman of the Theology Department and the instructor for several of my other classes during my freshman and sophomore years.

During my first two years, I enjoyed my theology classes, but honestly they did not excite me. Although the instructors were well versed in the subjects they taught and excellent teachers, for some reason there was no spark inside of me from the classes. In fact, many times, like some college students, I would catch myself nodding off during a lecture. My two favorite instructors were Dr. G.H. Surrette (Old Testament) and Dr. Jerry Horner (New Testament).

After four semesters of school, I was a passenger in a car involved in an automobile accident. It took a few months to fully recover from my injuries and I had to leave school. During that time, I became the pastor of a rural Baptist church and after a couple of years decided I needed to return to Southwest Baptist University and complete my studies. Upon returning, I found I had several classes with Dr. Jerry Horner as my instructor and I remembered how I used to nod off in his classes. Once again, it was not because he was not a good instructor, but I just didn't have the spark of enthusiasm in my theology courses I thought I should have.

I will never forget the first day of sitting in his class upon returning to school. The class was a study of the book of Hebrews and it was a ninety-minute class. Through the entire class session I sat on the edge of my seat and hung on every word, and when the ninety minutes were over, it seemed like it had only been a few minutes. Something had happened! Something had changed! There was something different about this instructor.

As the weeks passed, I could not get enough of his teaching. It was as though rivers of living water were flowing out of him. Back in those days, we used cassette recorders and I recorded every session. I listened to his teachings over and over and over again. I needed to know what had happened to Dr. Horner.

One day, between classes, I saw him in the student union and challenged him to a game of table tennis. As a college professor, he had a reputation of being a very good player, but I knew I was pretty good, too. After a close game (I can't remember who won), while we were laughing, I asked him this question. I said, "Dr. Horner, when I took your classes while attending school here before, they were just classes. But sitting under your teaching now, I cannot get enough. Your teaching has life to it. It's exciting. Something has changed. What has happened to you?"

The Power of Miracle Testimonies

It was at that point he shared two miraculous testimonies that had recently happened in his life. In one story, he related how he was traveling late at night on a holiday weekend in his foreign sports car. In those days, it was rare to find any garage that would repair a foreign car, much less at night on a holiday weekend. He related to me how his car was running so poorly that night, it would barely make it up the hills. He told the Lord, "This is probably my fault due to my negligence of not having the car serviced. But Lord, if you will get me home tonight, I promise I will have the car serviced properly as soon as the dealership opens after the weekend."

He said immediately the car began to run perfectly. I remember him saying it ran so perfectly that in his mind he was wondering if he actually needed to get it serviced. But he decided to keep his promise to the Lord, so after arriving safely home, he drove his foreign sports car in for repair the next day.

As he was waiting for his automobile to be serviced, the mechanic came up and asked Dr. Horner who had towed the car in for him. When the mechanic was told it was driven in, he said, "That's impossible! The rotor has been broken for some time and the engine is cool. The engine in the vehicle has not been running." When Dr. Horner told me this, I felt an excitement I had never felt before. ✳

Then he told me a second story of a time he was preaching at an event. In the crowd there were two girls who were making fun of God. In fact, one of them had a Coke bottle and was mocking God by saying that she could just put God in a bottle and seal Him off. As she said this, she stuck her finger in the bottle and then couldn't get her finger out.

People were coming forward for ministry, and these girls, still somewhat mocking but also in despair as the finger was swelling inside the bottle, came forward. Eventually they made their way onto the platform and the girl laid her hand and the bottle on Dr. Horner's hands. As he commanded her finger to be released from the bottle, he saw her finger dematerialize in the bottle and then rematerialize outside the bottle.

As he was telling me this story, he looked me in the eye and said, "This is why as you minister and make commands by the Holy Spirit, you want to keep your eyes open." He said, "If my eyes had been closed, I would have thought she somehow slipped her finger out of the bottle. But because my eyes were open and I was watching her hand, I saw her finger dematerialize and rematerialize."

Then he said, "Many more things have happened, but I'll have to tell you later because I have to get to class."

During this time in my life, as I said before, I was the pastor of a church, working in our family marine business, and attending the university full time with a full load of courses, all at the same time. I was also married, had two children, and I was living at home. The church was about 40 miles north of my home and the university was 100 miles south of where I lived. This means I spent a lot of time in my car every week and as I was driving, I listened to the teachings of Dr. Horner.

Seeing for Myself

I prayed that if these miracles were true, I wanted to be a person who could experience them. If healing was for today, I didn't just want to hear about someone's friend who knew somebody in Omaha that got healed. I wanted to see the healing first hand. If casting out demons was actually real, I didn't want to just hear about it, I wanted to see it. If miracles were not a thing of the past, but truly existed today, I wanted to see them happen.

Although I knew Jesus said it was more blessed to believe without seeing (John 20:29), I was in a place in my life where I needed to see something supernatural. I had spent my life going to church and hearing testimonies, but the greatest miracles I had ever heard were of how someone miraculously found a parking spot on a busy shopping day or how a headache had gone away. While it is true that God takes care of small things, I wanted to see His power manifested to a greater degree.

Because I commuted to school, I wasn't aware that Dr. Jerry Horner had taken the position as Chairman of the Theology Department at Oral Roberts University and would be leaving at the end of the semester. When I found out he was leaving SBU, and since he had become my favorite professor, I decided to invite him to our house during the summer break for a going away celebration. I also invited three other Baptist pastors who were attending the university, along with their spouses. Our house was on the lake, so everyone enjoyed the day swimming, boating, and cooking out.

As it began to get dark and people were starting to leave, one of the ministers made a comment about how he believed Melchizedek was the Christ. Well, immediately everyone got their Bibles out of their cars and a Bible study started in our living room. As Dr. Horner taught us, the topic changed to healing in the Bible.

One of the pastor's wives had an eye that was turned sideways in the socket, and it had been this way all of her life. As the Bible study progressed near midnight, Dr. Horner asked her if she would like to be healed. He placed his hand a few inches in front of her face and, without touching her, in a normal voice he simply said, "In the name of Jesus, be healed." When he removed his hand, both of her eyes were straight and normal.

I knew her husband very well from college. I immediately asked him to come with me into the kitchen and I said, "Tell me the truth. I don't want any exaggeration. Has your wife ever been able to hold her eye straight since you have known her?" He said, "Honestly, one time she tried to hold her eye straight. She never did accomplish it, but it gave her a headache so severe that she had to go to the doctor. The doctor told her, 'Don't you ever try to hold that eye straight again. It will never move and it could actually cause greater harm.'" I went back into the living room and both of her eyes were still straight.

I invited them back two weeks later for watermelon to see if her eye was still straight. It was. She was totally healed.

The Turning Point

When I saw this miraculous healing take place, I completely submitted to the things of God and to the Holy Spirit. Now my heart yearned for more. In my long hours of driving, I had been telling God, "If there is anything else, I want it." I even remember once saying, "Even speaking in tongues, if it is of You, I want it." I could barely get those words out of my mouth, but my heart was sincere. If tongues were of God, I wanted them!

At that moment, my desire to receive the supernatural manifestation of everything available from God became greater than the fear imparted by my denomination and confusing religious experiences of the past. That moment became the turning point when God began to pour out His Spirit in my life.

That night as I stood before Dr. Jerry Horner, he placed his hands on my head and he said something about receiving the Holy Spirit. I'm not sure exactly what he said, but I do know that words came out of my mouth and they were not in English. I remember him telling me later that he heard me speaking in ancient Hebrew and Greek as I was praising God.

My life changed that night. My preaching and teaching changed that night. My passion changed that night and now, over forty years later, the fire is still burning inside of me. I was saved, born again, and going to heaven at the age of seven. But as a young, married college student, I received the gift of the Promise (Acts 1:4) and I've never been the same since. Truly receiving the Holy Spirit is a powerful, life-changing second experience.

CHAPTER 7

THE NINE GIFTS OF THE SPIRIT

Now concerning spiritual gifts, brethren, I do not
want you to be ignorant... There are diversities of gifts,
but the same Spirit. There are differences of ministries, but the same Lord. And there are diversities of
activities, but it is the same God who works all in all.

But the manifestation of the Spirit is given to each
one for the profit of all: for to one is given the word
of wisdom through the Spirit, to another the word of
knowledge through the same Spirit, to another faith
by the same Spirit, to another gifts of healings by the
same Spirit, to another the working of miracles, to
another prophecy, to another discerning of spirits,
to another different kinds of tongues, to another the
interpretation of tongues.

But one and the same Spirit works all these things,
distributing to each one individually as He wills.

1 Corinthians 12:1, 4-11

As Christians, God has given to us the availability of the greatest power in the universe. This power can overcome any enemy or any obstacle that stands in the way of our complete victory. This power is the Holy Spirit, who is the Spirit of God. Since God is love, that makes the Holy Spirit the Spirit of love.

To equip us for this victory, the Holy Spirit has presented to the church nine spiritual gifts that cover every aspect of life. As we learn about the supernatural, spiritual things of the Holy Spirit, we cannot allow ourselves to ignore the study of His Word, or allow ourselves to neglect the duties that are clearly given in the Scriptures to the church.

> **Study to shew thyself approved unto God, a workman that needeth not to be ashamed, rightly dividing the word of truth.**
>
> **2 Timothy 2:15 (KJV)**

While God does not intend for us to rely on learned knowledge alone, through Bible study, worship, and prayer, we create an atmosphere for the Holy Spirit to reveal supernatural truth and wisdom from the scriptures we already have in our hearts.

As we study what the Word of God says concerning these gifts and as we meditate on the Scriptures, allow the Holy Spirit to reveal Himself to you. While we will categorize and list these gifts, we must never be rigid and dogmatic concerning the flow of the Spirit. The Holy Spirit is not rigid or abrasive, but the gifts flow as a river of living water to us and through us for the benefit of all. So relax, take a deep breath, and enjoy the revelation of the Word of God as the Holy Spirit teaches us.

Varieties of Gifts

"Now there are varieties of gifts, but the same Spirit. And there are varieties of ministries, and the same Lord. There are varieties of effects, but the same God who works all things in all persons" (1 Corinthians 12:4-6 NASB).

While there are varieties of gifts, ministries, and effects, we must remember it is the same God who works all these things in every person that is involved in a manifestation of the Spirit. Although these gifts are given individually, the purpose of the manifestation is for the common good of everyone involved.

Here is a listing of the nine gifts in the order they occur in the Bible:

1. The word of wisdom
2. The word of knowledge
3. Faith
4. Gifts of healings
5. The working of miracles
6. Prophecy
7. Discerning of spirits
8. Different kinds of tongues
9. The interpretation of tongues

While the above gifts are listed in this order in the Bible, they are not necessarily in order of importance. The Holy Spirit who works all of these gifts distributes each gift individually to whom He desires as He wills (1 Corinthians 12:11).

The gifts of the Holy Spirit always work together in unison and never conflict with each other. Many times a gift is used in conjunction with and blends with other gifts, but they will always work together for the same purpose.

Before we go any further, I would like to give a basic definition of each of the nine gifts.

1. The Gift of the Word of Wisdom
   This is the supernatural revelation by the Holy Spirit concerning the divine purpose and will of God.

2. The Gift of the Word of Knowledge
   This gift is the supernatural revelation by the Holy Spirit concerning knowledge from the mind of God.

3. The Gift of Faith
   The gift of faith is the supernatural endowment by the Holy Spirit when God increases the faith of a specific believer for a specific purpose and miraculously fulfills that purpose.

4. The Gifts of Healings
   These gifts are to deliver the sick and afflicted and to destroy the works of the devil in the human body.

5. The Gift of the Working of Miracles
   The gift of the working of miracles is the supernatural suspension of the course of nature and

physics to manifest the impossible in the realm of the physical through the Spirit of God.

6. The Gift of Prophecy
   The gift of prophecy is a supernatural utterance of things of God in a known language.

7. The Gift of the Discerning of Spirits
   Discerning of spirits is the ability to see into the spirit world and understand the source and purpose of a spirit.

8. The Gift of Different Kinds of Tongues
   This is the supernatural utterance by the Holy Spirit in languages never learned by the speaker or understood by the mind of the speaker, and not necessarily understood by the hearer.

9. The Gift of the Interpretation of Tongues
   This gift is the supernatural explanation by the Holy Spirit of the meaning of an utterance in an unknown tongue that is in an understandable language to the hearer.

The Three Groups

God has given the church special gifts that are administered by the Holy Spirit that meet different needs within the church. The purpose of all the gifts is to edify and build up the body of Christ (1 Corinthians 14:12). The gifts of the Spirit can be divided into three basic groups or categories which will help in the understanding of these gifts. They are the gifts of speech, the gifts of power, and the gifts of revelation.

gifts of speech

The first group is the gifts of speech. They are prophecy, different kinds of tongues, and interpretation of tongues. All three of these gifts say something through the anointing of the Holy Spirit.

The second group is the gifts of power. Likewise, there are three gifts in this group. They are the gift of faith, the working of miracles, and the gifts of healings. These gifts perform an act, or we could say, these gifts do something.

The third group is the gifts of revelation. They are the word of wisdom, the word of knowledge, and discerning of spirits. The revelation gifts each reveal something.

All nine of these gifts are distributed by the Holy Spirit and remember, He distributes them to each one individually according to His will.

A. The Gifts of Speech (They say something)
- Prophecy
- Different Kinds of Tongues
- Interpretation of Tongues

Holy Spirit Speak

B. The Gifts of Power (They do something)
- The Gift of Faith
- The Working of Miracles
- The Gifts of Healings

perform an act

C. The Gifts of Revelation (They reveal something)
- The Word of Wisdom
- The Word of Knowledge
- Discerning of Spirits

The Parallel Flow

Generally speaking, there is a parallel flow of the nine spiritual gifts. While the phrase *parallel flow* is not used in the Bible, the concept is woven throughout the instructions to the New Testament church. In the same way that the word *trinity* and the word *rapture* are not found in the Bible but their concepts are clearly shown, so it is with the parallel flow of the gifts. Let me explain exactly what I mean.

Every believer who is a part of the church has authority over the power of the enemy and has been authorized to heal the sick, raise the dead, and cast out demons (Mark 16:17). A Christian can do this of their own free will by taking the authority that has been given and using it as they see necessary. These actions involve healing, miracles, and authority and are to be a part of the work that every Christian has been commissioned to do through faith.

On the other hand, the gifts of the Holy Spirit are distributed to a believer who has asked to receive the Holy Spirit and has been filled with the eventual evidence of speaking in tongues. While through these gifts healings and miracles occur, the difference is they are at the direction of the Holy Spirit in His timing and by His desire.

For example, wisdom is obtained by asking God (James 1:5). The word of wisdom is a gift of the Spirit (1 Corinthians 12:8). Knowledge is obtained by study of the Word (2 Timothy 2:15). The word of knowledge is a gift of the Spirit (1 Corinthians 12:8). Faith is obtained by hearing the Word (Romans 10:17). The gift of faith is a gift of the Spirit (1 Cor-

Wisdom

Knowledge

Faith

inthians 12:9). Praying in the spirit is a result of your desire to pray God's will in tongues (1 Corinthians 14:2). The gift of different kinds of tongues is a gift of the Holy Spirit that is distributed as He wills (1 Corinthians 12:10-11).

The parallel flow of tongues is different from the other gifts, because speaking in tongues signifies the filling of the Holy Spirit Himself. While the natural flow of healings, miracles, knowledge, and faith are available to all believers, praying in the spirit and all types of tongues both occur only after a person has asked and received the filling of the Holy Spirit.

Learning to Flow in the Gifts

For every mature saint of God who walks deeply in the manifestations of the Holy Spirit, there was an early time when they were learning to take their first spiritual steps. Sometimes these first steps can seem awkward and cause them to feel self-conscious.

I remember the first time I prayed in public at Spring Valley Baptist Church in Raytown, Missouri. I was twelve years old and although my prayer only consisted of a few lines, I was shaking inside all morning. But like everything else, we can mature in the things of God so that moving in the Holy Spirit will be as natural as breathing.

Learning to flow in the gifts of the Spirit could be likened to learning to ride a bicycle. I remember my daughter getting a bicycle for Christmas when she was a very young child. She wanted to ride it, oh so badly. It took a few weeks of practice with training wheels and with me instructing, and she took a few falls. Although she was a little wobbly at first, the time came when we took off the training wheels and she began to ride confidently on her own.

In the same way you will never learn to ride a bike without training and a few falls, it may take a while to learn to flow in the gifts of the Spirit. Mature Christians should understand this and not be critical but helpful. We would not criticize a toddler for not being able to run like a teenager; likewise, we should never criticize spiritual toddlers.

Flowing in the Spirit requires not only desire, but training and practice to move past the fear of failure or embarrassment of falling. While correction may need to be done, it should always be bathed with love and never be critical or sarcastic.

As a young child praying at church, had I allowed the fear of getting in front of people to stop me, I would have never learned to pray in public which would have definitely hindered my call in the ministry!

For everything in life there is a first time followed by training. The Holy Spirit is the teacher who reveals the Word of God. Experience is not the teacher but through practice we gain experience. With revelation by the Holy Spirit and experience, we develop the skill and ability that's required to be mature in the gifts of the Holy Spirit.

One Step at a Time

Many times while I am ministering, I don't know exactly what is going to happen or what gift is going to be in operation, but the Holy Spirit will tell me a step to take.

For example, a few weeks ago a gentleman was sitting in the congregation and the Holy Spirit spoke to me and told me to bring him up on the platform and pray for him. So I took that step. I brought him up to pray for him.

As he walked up the steps, the word of knowledge started coming up inside of me. I knew a few words of what I was to say, but I didn't know all of what I was supposed to say until I started saying it. As I was speaking, I was thinking, "This guy has a real problem. How is he going to solve it?"

The word of wisdom was getting ready to come up, but it hadn't started yet. God will take you a step at a time, but you must step out first in obedience. No matter how insignificant it may seem, we must be led by the Spirit. Sometimes the smallest of actions can yield the greatest results. Let Him guide you step by step.

Decently and in Order

Let all things be done decently and in order.
1 Corinthians 14:40

Because God is a God of order in all of His creation, the distribution of the gifts of the Holy Spirit will also follow order. Confusion and chaos will never be the result of the proper administration of the gifts.

The Holy Spirit will not interrupt Himself. Many of us have been in meetings where one person might be trying to prophesy and give a prophetic utterance to the congregation, while at the same time another person is trying to give a message in tongues. You can easily see the competition between the two people, each trying to speak louder than the other one so they can be heard.

But if the source of the prophetic word and the source of the message in tongues are both truly authentic, then they would be giftings from the same Spirit and the Holy Spirit will not interrupt Himself. There should never be competition with the gifts, and if there is, it is not of God.

> **If anyone speaks in a tongue, let there be two or at the most three, each in turn, and let one interpret... But if anything is revealed to another who sits by, let the first keep silent.**
>
> **1 Corinthians 14:27,30**

As a young Christian, I remember attending a tent revival and watching a great man and woman of God operating in the gifts together. One would speak in an unknown tongue and the other would interpret. They flowed so well in the Spirit together that everyone was edified and strengthened by the word from God to the congregation.

While there will always be those who are critical of the move of God and will ridicule as on the Day of Pentecost, we cannot allow the words of the world to hinder us or cause us to quench the work of the Holy Spirit. As we are led by the Spirit, the gifts will flow properly and in accordance with order.

Let's now examine each of the nine gifts in greater detail.

CHAPTER 8

THE GIFT OF THE WORD OF WISDOM
First Gift

**But the manifestation of the Spirit is given to each
one for the profit of all: for to one is given the word
of wisdom through the Spirit...**

1 Corinthians 12:7-8

D*efinition:* The gift of the word of wisdom is the supernatural revelation by the Holy Spirit concerning the
divine purpose and will of God.

One of the nine gifts of the Holy Spirit is called the word
of wisdom. This gift is wisdom from God imparted by the
Holy Spirit that is beyond natural human comprehension. It
is speaking wisdom from the Spirit of God into someone's
life without the speaker knowing what is going to be said to
the person receiving the word.

The Parallel Flow

Wisdom from God for everyday life is always available to
every born-again believer. The Book of James is a letter that

was written to all Christians. In James 1:5 it says, *"If any of you lacks wisdom, let him ask of God who gives to all liberally without reproach, and it will be given to him."* This verse tells us that a Christian who lacks natural wisdom can receive wisdom in abundance from God and all he must do is ask in faith and receive it.

However, the Bible tells us of a supernatural anointing of wisdom called the word of wisdom. First Corinthians 12:8 lists it as one of the nine gifts of the Holy Spirit.

What is the difference between natural wisdom from God and the gift of the word of wisdom? Actually, the answer is simple. Natural wisdom that is available to the born-again believer is wisdom that can be used in making the day-to-day decisions in life. This wisdom can be used in natural affairs and in ministry affairs and it is available for the asking. However, the word of wisdom is only available to a believer who has been filled with the Holy Spirit and this gift is given only as the Spirit wills to distribute it.

Understanding the Difference

When talking about the things of God, it is very important to name them as God names them. When something is not named properly, it brings confusion to the hearer. If I called an automobile an airplane, then all of our discussion about my travel would be confusing because I would be speaking of one thing and you would be picturing something else. Likewise, when interpreting scripture, we can eliminate confusion by understanding God's wording. A definition means nothing unless you clearly know the word it is defining.

With that in mind, we must understand there is a difference between natural wisdom and the word of wisdom. A word is not a complete sentence. A word is only a portion of a sentence. Likewise, although God has all knowledge and all wisdom because there is nothing that He does not know, He does not reveal all of His knowledge or wisdom, but only a portion or a word. It is the *gift of the word of wisdom* and not the *gift of wisdom*. To say the *gift of wisdom* implies that all wisdom has been attained, but the *word of wisdom* implies that God is imparting a portion of His wisdom that is necessary for the benefit of the hearer.

As an example, if you were needing medical advice, a doctor would only give you the portion pertaining to your request, but would not tell you all of his wisdom that he had attained in his many years of medical study. Likewise, God imparts the word of wisdom necessary for our benefit.

The word of wisdom and the word of knowledge are often gifts that operate together, but they are distinctly different in that the word of knowledge deals with present or past facts or events, while the word of wisdom points toward the future.

A New Testament Example

While Saul was on the road to Damascus to persecute Christians, a bright light shone from heaven. Jesus spoke to him out of light and said, *"Saul, Saul, why are you persecuting me?"* (v.7). Saul said, *"Who are You Lord?"* and Jesus said to Him, *"I am Jesus of Nazareth whom you are persecuting"* (v.8).

Later, as Paul recounts this event, he said the men who were traveling with him were afraid and saw the light, *"but they did not hear the voice of Him who spoke to me"* (v.9). The phrase "did not hear" in the Greek is *ouk ēkousan* which is a verb to be taken in the sense of "not understood."

In other words, those with Saul heard but did not understand the words of Jesus. Saul did, and he responded to Jesus by asking Him what he should do. Jesus told him, *"Arise and go into Damascus and there you will be told all things which are appointed for you to do"* (v.10).

Because Saul was blinded by the glory of the light, those who were with him had to lead him by his hand to Damascus. (Acts 22:4-11.)

While he was staying in Damascus, there was a disciple of the Lord Jesus named Ananias who had a vision. In the vision the Lord Jesus spoke to him by name and gave him instruction. He told him, *"Arise and go to the Street called Strait, and inquire at the house of Judas for one called Saul of Tarsus, for behold, he is praying. And in a vision he has seen a man named Ananias coming in and putting his hand on him, so that he might receive his sight"* (vv.11-12).

Of course, Ananias knew Saul of Tarsus had an infamous reputation of imprisoning and torturing Christians in Jerusalem and he also knew Saul had authority from the chief priests to arrest anyone who called themselves a Christian, and in the vision he shared this with the Lord. But the Lord said to him, *"Go, for he is a chosen vessel of Mine to bear My name before Gentiles, kings, and the children of Israel. For I will*

show him how many things he must suffer for My name's sake"
(vv.15-16).

After his vision with the Lord, Ananias went to the place as instructed by the word of the Lord. He laid hands on Saul and told him that the Lord Jesus had appeared to him and sent him so that Saul would receive his sight and be filled with the Holy Spirit. Immediately something like scales fell from the eyes of Saul and at that very moment he received his sight. Saul was baptized and spent many days with the disciples at Damascus. (Acts 9:10-19.)

This account in the book of Acts reveals the word of wisdom and the word of knowledge in operation. Ananias was told exactly where to find Saul and he was told Saul had been praying and that he had received a vision. The exact street and location of the house was revealed. It was also revealed to Ananias by the Holy Spirit that Saul had seen a man called Ananias lay hands on him and that he would be healed.

The revelation of these things were all things that had already happened. The only way Ananias could have known of these events would be by revelation of the Holy Spirit. This was the word of knowledge in operation.

But when Ananias was told in his vision what to say to Saul about being a chosen vessel to bear the name of the Lord before Gentiles, kings, and the children of Israel, that was not something that *had* happened, but something that *would* happen and this revelation was the word of wisdom in operation. Remember, the word of knowledge is supernatural revelation of the present or past and the word of wisdom brings revelation of future events.

God revealed to Ananias, through a vision, events that had taken place in the life of Saul (the word of knowledge) and God's plan for Saul in the future (the word of wisdom).

Operating in the Word of Wisdom

Several years ago, I was asked to speak to some business people in our local town. The meeting took place in a banquet room at a local bank. They asked me to come and speak what was on my heart. The things of God are always on my heart.

Although I was in the ministry at the time, I was also the president of the Lake of the Ozarks Marine Dealers Association and chairman of the State Marine Board. They probably thought I was going to talk about high performance power boats, but I didn't. I talked about the things of God and after I spoke, I had an altar call. The business people were very receptive. I laid hands on many people and prayed with them.

Near the end of the meeting, one of the local business women came forward. I had never seen the lady before that night. I asked her what she would like to receive from the Lord and she said she wanted God to help her quit smoking. I agreed with her in prayer that she would receive the strength to quit. But as she turned away and started walking toward the back of the meeting room, the Spirit of God came upon me and imparted to me the word of knowledge and the word of wisdom.

I called to the lady. She turned and said, "Yes?" I heard myself saying, "The Spirit of God would say to you this night, if you would take the cigarettes you have hidden inside the vase by the couch, the cigarettes you've hidden in the cannister in the cabinet above the sink in your kitchen, and the cigarettes you've hidden in the drawer..."

My mind was thinking, "What am I saying?" For all I knew this lady didn't even have a vase beside her couch, or a couch for that matter, but the Holy Spirit had given me three specific places where she had hidden cigarettes. This information was being imparted to me as supernatural knowledge or the word of knowledge. They were facts about her life I had no way of knowing. No education in any institution of higher learning in the world could have taught me what I was speaking boldly as fact.

Then I continued as the word of wisdom came out: "If you will take those cigarettes that you've hidden in those three places, crumble them up, but don't burn them, and throw them away, you will be delivered of smoking permanently." I could see her face turn white as she turned toward me and acknowledged that what I said was true. But then she made a startling statement. She said, "I can't do that because cigarettes are expensive and when I start smoking again, I'll just have to go and buy new ones." She was already planning to get back into what she was asking God to deliver her from!

God loved this lady so much that He imparted the word of knowledge to me to reveal a truth in her life. By revealing this supernatural knowledge of things I could not have known, she would know that she was hearing from God. And then He imparted the word of wisdom to me on how to solve the problem. She rejected the wisdom of God. Through her rejection of the word of wisdom, it exposed what was in her heart. She was asking God to deliver her from smoking, but she had no intention of getting delivered.

The wisdom that comes from God through the impartation of the word of wisdom by the Holy Spirit is supernatural wisdom beyond the wisdom of men and wisdom that cannot be attained by intellect or experience.

So the bottom line is this. As a Christian, we should be asking God for wisdom daily and be ready and willing to receive the word of wisdom as He imparts it to us by His Holy Spirit.

Visions, Dreams, and the Spoken Word

According to Scripture, the word of wisdom can come through a vision, a dream, or the spoken word. The word of wisdom can also come through the gift of prophecy or through the gift of tongues and interpretation. However we must remember that the wisdom of future events is the word of wisdom and not the gift of prophecy itself. First Corinthians 14:3 tells us the gift of prophecy is spoken to men for a specific purpose and that purpose is edification, exhortation, and comfort. There is no revelation in the gift of prophecy, but if a revelation comes through the prophecy, it is actually the gift of the word of knowledge or the word of wisdom.

In the New Testament church there was a prophet named Agabus. After traveling from Jerusalem to Antioch, he stood up and by the Spirit said there was going to be a great famine throughout all the world, which happened while Claudius

Caesar was Emperor of Rome. The disciples believed the words spoken by him and each, according to their own ability, determined they would send relief to the brethren that were dwelling in Judea. After gathering the relief items together, they sent the items to the elders by way of Barnabas and Saul. Obviously, Agabus was a man of character and integrity and had proven himself. (Acts 11:27-30.)

Another time Agabus, after having traveled from Judea, took Paul's belt and bound his own hands and feet and said, *"Thus says the Holy Spirit, 'so shall the Jews at Jerusalem bind the man that owns this belt, and deliver him into the hands of the Gentiles'"* (vs. 11). When the disciples heard this, they pleaded with Paul not to go up to Jerusalem, but Paul said, *"What do you mean by weeping and breaking my heart? For I am ready not only to be bound, but also to die at Jerusalem for the name of the Lord Jesus"* (vs.13). And after they realized they could not change the mind of Paul, they simply said, *"The will of the Lord be done"* (vs.14). And within a few days they packed their belongings and went up to Jerusalem. (Acts 21:10-15.)

Although Agabus was a prophet, he was not speaking edification, exhortation, and comfort to men as prophecy, but was speaking the word of wisdom concerning future events. In one case, the future event was related to weather conditions and in another case, the future event was related to the actions of men. Only through the revealed wisdom of God could he know of these events and only by yielding to the gift of the word of wisdom would he be able to speak them. In the case of the drought to come and in the case of the actions of men, the revelation was so they could prepare for it.

Rejecting the Word of Wisdom Can be Costly

When Paul was traveling by ship to Rome to meet with Caesar, he advised the centurion during the voyage by saying, *"Men, I perceive that this voyage will end with disaster and much loss, not only of the cargo and ship, but also our lives"* (vs.10). When the centurion heard this, he was more persuaded by the owner and helmsman of the ship than by what Paul had spoken. Because the harbor was not a suitable place to stay in winter, the majority convinced the helmsman to leave and winter in Phoenix, a harbor of Crete.

While the wind blew softly and it appeared that they had obtained their purpose, they sailed close to Crete. But suddenly a great head wind arose so that the ship was caught and could not head into the wind. Fearing that they would run aground and because the waves of the sea were so great, the next day they lightened the load. On the third day of this storm, they threw the ship's tackle overboard. Eventually the crew lost all hope and gave up.

After a long time of going without food and in great despair, Paul stood up in the middle of those on board and said, *"Men, you should have listened to me, and not have sailed from Crete and incurred this disaster and loss. And now I urge you to take heart for there will be no loss of life among you, but only the ship. For there stood by me this night an angel of the God to whom I belong and whom I serve, saying, 'Do not be afraid, Paul; you must be brought before Caesar; and indeed God has granted you all those who sail with you.' Therefore, take heart, men, for I believe God that it will be just as it was told me. However, we must run aground on a certain island"* (vv. 21-26).

Later, when it looked like the ship was going to run aground, some of the sailors tried to let down the skiff and escape the ship, but Paul told the centurion and the soldiers that unless they stayed on the ship with him, they could not be saved. The soldiers cut the ropes to the skiff and everyone stayed on the ship. The ship later ran aground and was broken up by the violence of the waves. Some swam to the land and others floated to shore on boards and broken pieces of the ship, but the end result was that all 276 people (v. 37) on the ship escaped safely to land and survived. (Acts 27:10-44.)

When Paul spoke by the Spirit and told the centurion not to set sail, the centurion did not follow the instructions of the Holy Spirit given by Paul and they encountered a great storm. The second time that Paul spoke by the Spirit of the Lord and said that if they would stay on the ship, they would all be saved, the centurion listened to the word of the Lord through Paul and not one of the 276 persons on board lost their lives.

This reveals a very important detail about the word of wisdom. Since it is looking forward toward future events that have not taken place, choices must be made on whether or not to heed the word of the Lord. The word of wisdom, like the other eight gifts of the Holy Spirit, is for the benefit and profit of everyone involved. But this is only the case when the word of God that has been spoken is obeyed.

The Word of Wisdom Imparted to the Church

However, when He, the Spirit of truth, has come, He will guide you into all truth; for He will not speak on His own authority, but whatever He hears He will speak; and He will tell you things to come.

John 16:13

When Jesus gave His disciples the information that He would be leaving and instructed them in great detail concerning the promise of the Holy Spirit, He told them that when the Holy Spirit was imparted by the Father, that He, the Holy Spirit, would reveal things to come. In this verse, Jesus prophesied the manifestation of the word of wisdom would be imparted to the church by the Holy Spirit.

The Holy Spirit knows your need and has the wisdom for that need to be met. He desires fulfillment of every promise in our lives. As we yield to His Spirit, He will impart the word of wisdom that, when followed, will bring deliverance.

CHAPTER 9

THE GIFT OF THE WORD OF KNOWLEDGE
Second Gift

But the manifestation of the Spirit is given to each one for the profit of all ... to another the word of knowledge through the same Spirit ...

1 Corinthians 12:7,8

Definition: The gift of the word of knowledge is the supernatural revelation by the Holy Spirit concerning knowledge from the mind of God.

The second gift listed in First Corinthians 12 is the gift of the word of knowledge. With this gift, a portion of knowledge from God is imparted to a Spirit-filled believer for the purpose of revealing a truth or fact that would otherwise be unknown.

The Parallel Flow

Through my many years of ministry, I have known and developed friendships with many Bible scholars, Bible teachers, university professors, and people with high degrees of learning. I respect those who have earned degrees and have shown themselves diligent in the study of God's Word. After all, Second Timothy 2:15 (KJV) says we should study to show ourselves approved.

But regardless of the depth of knowledge obtained by natural study of the Word of God, we cannot confuse the attained knowledge and intellect of man with the word of knowledge. We must always remember the word of knowledge is a supernatural gift. When we study the Word of God, whether privately, in a classroom setting, or in a ministry service, the Holy Spirit reveals that Word to a greater depth within our heart, and as the depth of the Word is revealed or made *rhema* in our hearts, faith grows.

The study of God's Word by a believer can bring great revelation by the Holy Spirit; however, this is not the gift of the word of knowledge. The gift of the word of knowledge reveals a truth or a fact that cannot be obtained by any earthly study, but can only be revealed by the Holy Spirit at His direction.

The Holy Spirit Knows Where You Left Your Keys

For nothing is secret that will not be revealed, nor anything hidden that will not be known and come to light.

Luke 8:17

While the Bible tells us that the Holy Spirit can show us things to come, He can also reveal things that are lost. Something as simple as finding the keys to your car can be revealed by the Holy Spirit.

We must never forget that the Holy Spirit knows everything. Because He knows where every atom is located in the universe, He certainly knows where the keys to your automobile are that you can't find. So, if you cannot find something you need, then pray to the Father and through His Spirit, hidden or lost things will be revealed.

Operating in the Word of Knowledge

In Acts chapter 5, there was a man named Ananias who, along with his wife, Sapphira, sold some land. When they sold the land, they kept back a certain amount of the money for themselves. Ananias took the balance and gave it to Peter and the apostles, who were the leaders of the early church.

When he laid the money at the feet of the apostles, Peter said, *"Ananias, why has Satan filled your heart to lie to the Holy Spirit and keep back part of the price of the land for yourself? While it remained, was it not your own? And after it was sold, was it not in your own control? Why have you conceived this thing in your heart? You have not lied to men but to God"* (Acts 5:3-4).

When Ananias heard these words he fell down dead. Later, his wife came in and the same thing happened to her (vv. 7-10). How did Peter know they had kept some of the money? The answer is, Peter didn't know, but the Holy Spirit did. Peter, who had been filled with the Holy Spirit, was operating in the gift of the word of knowledge. There was no way he could have known, but the Holy Spirit, who is the Spirit of God, knows everything. Nothing is hidden from God.

Imparting the Word of Knowledge

Several years ago, my wife, Loretta, and I were speaking at a series of meetings in Iowa. At the end of one of these meetings, a man and woman came to the front of the congregation and asked us to pray for them. I asked them what they would like us to agree in prayer with them and they indicated they needed help in the area of finances. It seemed that even though they both worked, their finances never seemed to stretch to the weekend. Instead of having money left over at the end of the week, they had week left over at the end of the money.

Well, just as I started to pray, Loretta quickly looked up and said, "Are you two married?" I looked down at their hands and they were both wearing wedding rings. I thought to myself, "Oops! Loretta really missed it this time."

The man and woman both looked up and had strange looks on their faces. The man said, "Well, yes, of course, we're married." Then he paused and said, "But not to each other."

Loretta had hit the nail on the head. These two people were living in adultery and asking God to bless them.

How Did They Know?

But here's the question. How did Loretta know these two people were not married to each other? We had never been to that church before. We had never even been to that town before.

Well, here's the answer. Loretta didn't know, but the Holy Spirit did. In the same way that Peter knew the land was sold for more money than Ananias and Sapphira had said, Loretta knew the couple wasn't married. These secrets were revealed to Loretta and Peter by the same Holy Spirit through the word of knowledge.

Even though these events happened 2,000 years apart, it was the same Holy Spirit revealing this hidden knowledge to both of them. God's power has not diminished. He is no less supernatural today than He was 2,000 years ago.

The Visions of Cornelius and Peter

In Caesarea there was a Gentile named Cornelius, who was a centurion in the Italian regiment of the Roman army. He was a devout man who feared God and was generous to the poor. Every day he prayed regularly to the God of Abraham, Isaac, and Jacob. One day while praying about 3 o'clock in the afternoon, he had a clear vision where he saw an angel of God come to him and call him by name.

As he observed and questioned the angel in this vision, the angel spoke to him and said, *"Your prayers and your alms have come up for a memorial before God. Now send men to Joppa and send for Simon whose surname is Peter. He is lodging with Simon, a tanner, whose house is by the sea. He will tell you what you must do"* (vv. 4-6). When the angel who spoke to him departed from his vision, Cornelius called two of his servants and a third man, who was a devout soldier. After explaining the vision to these three men, he sent them to Joppa.

The next day they went on their journey, about noon as they were drawing near the city, Peter went up on the house-top to pray. Peter became very hungry and wanted to eat. As his host was preparing the meal, he fell into a trance where he saw heaven open up. An object like a great sheet bound at the four corners descended to him out of heaven to the earth. In this great sheet were all kinds of four-footed animals, wild beasts, creeping things, and birds of the air. Then a voice spoke to him and said, *"Rise, Peter; kill and eat"* (v.13). But Peter said, *"Not so, Lord! For I have never eaten anything common or unclean"* (v.14). And a voice spoke to him again a second time and said, *"What God has cleansed, you must not call common"* (v.15). This vision occurred three times and then the object was taken up into heaven again.

While Peter was perplexed about what this vision could possibly mean, the men who had been sent by Cornelius approached Simon's house and stood before the gate. As Peter was on the roof contemplating the vision, the Holy Spirit spoke to him and said, *"Behold, three men are seeking you. Arise therefore, go down and go with them, doubting nothing; for I have sent them"* (vv.19-20).

Immediately Peter went down from the roof and met the men that Cornelius had sent to him. After letting him know that he was the one they were seeking, he asked them why they had come to his house. They told him, *"Cornelius the centurion, a just man, one who fears God and has a good reputation among all the nations of the Jews was divinely instructed by a holy angel to summon you to his house to hear words from you"* (v.22). The very next day Peter left with them and took some of his brethren from Joppa to meet Cornelius. (Acts 10:1-23.)

Knowing the Unknown

This story of Peter's vision from the Lord and his obedience in going to the house of the Gentile, Cornelius, is a perfect example of the word of knowledge in operation. While Peter was on the roof, he was informed by the Holy Spirit that three men were waiting for him at the entrance to his house. This is a word of knowledge that would be impossible to know with the natural mind, but was revealed by the Holy Spirit. He was not only told that three men were at the front door, but he was told that the Holy Spirit had sent them. It was a revelation of something that had already taken place.

In the Bible, the word of knowledge was administered in a number of different ways—sometimes through the gift of prophecy, through tongues and interpretation, through a vision, a trance, or even an angel delivering a word of knowledge.

Although we have defined the gift of the word of wisdom and the gift of the word of knowledge separately, many times their usage is so intertwined that they appear to work as one. Working together, they reveal an unknown truth and give divine wisdom. But in the end, the Holy Spirit distributes and administers them in such a way that everyone receives benefit.

CHAPTER 10

THE GIFT OF FAITH
Third Gift

**But the manifestation of the Spirit is given to each one
for the profit of all ... to another faith by the same Spirit...**
1 Corinthians 12:7,9

Definition: The gift of faith is the supernatural endowment by the Holy Spirit when God increases the faith of a specific believer for a specific purpose and miraculously fulfills that purpose.

In Chapter 7, you will find where we have grouped the nine gifts of the Holy Spirit into three groups. One of the three groups is called the gifts of power. They are the gift of faith, the working of miracles, and the gifts of healings. The gift of faith is the greatest of the three power gifts. Faith is required for everything that happens in the life of a believer.

The Parallel Flow

The third gift of the Holy Spirit as listed in First Corinthians chapter twelve is the gift of faith. With the previous gifts of the Holy Spirit that we have covered, there is a parallel in the natural life of a Christian. So it is with the flow of faith. The natural flow of faith is faith that is available to every believer. This natural flow of faith comes by hearing and hearing by the Word of God. *"So then faith comes by hearing, and hearing by the word of God"* (Romans 10:17).

Everything we receive from God, we receive by faith. A perfect example is salvation. Ephesians 2:8 says, *"For by grace we have been saved through faith."* Grace is God's unmerited favor that empowers us to do the impossible. It is impossible for us to save ourselves. Faith is believing God so completely that all of our words and actions align with our belief in His promise. So we could say that we are saved by God's power through believing Him.

In John 3:16, Jesus clearly told us that God loved us so much that He sent His Son, and the only requirement for us to have everlasting life is to believe in Him. In other words, God would provide the eternal life through His power (grace) if man would only believe (have faith).

The template for receiving all of the promises of God is the simple act of faith. A man has faith for what God promised, then God physically provides something that man needs but does not have the ability to obtain on his own. Not only is it impossible to please Him without faith (Hebrews 11:6), but it is impossible to receive from Him without faith.

... Let us prophesy in proportion to our faith.

Romans 12:6

Sometimes the faith required for the miraculous is beyond the realm of natural faith. The Holy Spirit imparts the gift of faith so that the believer believes beyond their natural ability to believe, and the end result is miraculous deliverance.

How Natural Faith Grows

Natural faith can be measured. The Bible refers to little faith (Matthew 8:26) and great faith (Matthew 8:10). In fact, at one time the disciples of Jesus asked to have their faith increased (Luke 17:5). So obviously, faith is something that grows. How does it grow? Again Romans 10:17 says, *"So then faith comes by hearing and hearing by the word of God."*

In the natural life of all believers, faith is extremely important. Everything a Christian receives must be received by faith. Ephesians 2:8 tells us we are saved through faith. Hebrews 11:6 says that we need faith to please God. James 5:15 says the prayer of faith will heal the sick. James 1:6-7 says if we don't pray in faith, we won't receive anything. Then Romans 14:23 says that anything that is not of faith is sin and Hebrews 4:2 makes an astonishing statement. It says that without faith, the gospel is unprofitable, and First John 5:4 tells us that faith is our victory that overcomes the world.

Is faith important? Of course it is! According to the Bible, without faith we are lost, sick, in lack, in sin, unpleasing to God, defeated, and have a gospel that doesn't work. But do we have to live this way? No, we do not. Why? Because faith is available to every believer.

Faith comes by hearing and hearing by the Word of God. If we want faith, all we have to do is hear the Word and allow the Word to saturate our hearts. As we meditate on the Word, the Holy Spirit brings revelation, then the Word becomes *rhema*. With this revelation of the Word, faith grows.

What is *rhema*? The oldest manuscripts we have for the New Testament are in the Greek language and the Greek language has two words, *logos* and *rhema*, that are both translated into English as *word*. So when we read a scripture like Romans 10:17 that says faith comes by hearing the Word of God, we can only tell by looking at the Greek text whether the word is translated from *logos* or *rhema*.

Logos in its simplest form could be translated *written word*. *Rhema* means *spoken or revealed word*. The Greek word used in Romans 10:17 is *rhema*. This means that faith does not come by simply reading the written word, but when the written Word of God is revealed in your heart by the Holy Spirit. The only scripture in the entire Bible that tells how faith comes clearly says that it comes through revelation of the Word of God by the Holy Spirit.

So then faith comes by hearing, and hearing by the word of God.

Romans 10:17

The Gift of Faith

The second flow of faith is called the gift of faith. This special faith is limited to the will and distribution of the Holy Spirit.

The gift of faith cannot be measured. It is so powerful that doubt and unbelief do not exist in any degree. When the gift of faith is imparted, there is a full knowledge and understanding that the will of God and purpose of God will be fulfilled. There is no hesitation, wavering, or uncertainty in the person who receives and operates in the gift of faith.

The gift of faith is not received by asking and begging. It is imparted to the believer as the Holy Spirit desires and wills to do so. For every distribution of the gift of faith there is a purpose, and the Holy Spirit imparts this gift where it will not be quenched, but will fulfill the purpose for which it was given.

The Faith of One Man to Deliver a City

In an earlier chapter, we reviewed the Bible account of Philip going to Samaria and through his teaching about Christ, the entire city was born again. In the biblical account of this story in Acts chapter 8, it tells about the great healings and the great miracles that took place. It even specifically says that demons were cast out of people and that there were others who were completely paralyzed or crippled who were healed and restored to total health. (Acts 8:4-8.)

Then the apostles in Jerusalem sent Peter and John to Samaria to lay hands on these new Christians in order for them to receive the Holy Spirit. We are told very clearly in this passage that the Holy Spirit had fallen upon none of them until Peter and John arrived. (Acts 8:14-17.)

The point is this. All of the healings, all of the miracles, all of the casting out of demons took place before any of the people of Samaria had received the Holy Spirit. This tells us that all of the gifts of the Spirit were in operation through Philip—including the gift of faith. In this account, an entire city was delivered through the gifts of the Holy Spirit working through one man.

As Philip operated under the power and anointing of the Holy Spirit and as the gift of faith flowed through him, the only requirement of those who needed deliverance was for them to believe and receive. The Bible says as Philip preached Christ to them, the multitudes in Samaria heard and received the things he spoke and the result was deliverance.

Faith for a Miracle

Let me illustrate the gift of faith. Several years ago, Loretta and I went to Quincy, Illinois for a Saturday evening meeting in the student union of a university. The next morning I was to speak at one of the local churches and then we would go to the airport and fly home. Meetings like this were always a joy for me. Not only did I enjoy the meetings, but I enjoyed flying. In fact, I especially enjoyed flying to Quincy, Illinois. The airport was large with long and wide runways and very little traffic. Several times I flew to Quincy just to get a piece of lemon meringue pie à la mode at the little café in the terminal.

However, this ministry trip was different. It seemed like anything that could delay me, was delaying me. It took longer to get the airplane ready, there was the threat of storms, and by the time I got to the meeting, I was not in a good mood.

Quite honestly, that's not my nature. I've always had a reputation for being a happy guy. In fact, sometimes I'm so happy it irritates people. Anyway, as I was sitting on the platform waiting for the meeting to begin, a gentleman in his fifties slowly came through the back door. His arm and back were twisted, one leg was turned so much that it looked backwards, and his head was tilted to one side.

It almost embarrasses me to admit this, but as he walked in the back of the auditorium, my attitude was so poor that under my breath I said, "God, don't let this man come forward for healing!"

A friend of mine, who is a senator, had received a flyer saying that I was going to be in Quincy. Although he couldn't attend the meeting, he encouraged a friend of his who was a businessman from the Middle East to come, and he did. As the music and meeting progressed, there was an anointing from God that came into the auditorium that changed the atmosphere and my attitude. The Middle East businessman got very excited about the word for healing that I was sharing. Although he had never seen the crippled man before, as soon as the invitation was given, he grabbed him, brought him forward, and stood in the line next to him.

People were lined up all across the front of the auditorium. As I looked at the crippled man to my left, the Spirit of God imparted to me the gift of faith. This was not faith that had been built by me reading the Word, although I had been reading the Word. I KNEW this man would be healed.

Confidently, I walked to him. I calmly pointed my finger in his face and said, "If you will believe you can be healed, you will be healed." He looked at me and said, "I believe." I stretched out my hand to place it on his head, but his head was twisted so far to the side that I actually put my hand on his neck and I calmly said, "In the name of Jesus, be healed."

Over the years I've prayed for thousands to be healed. But the confidence I experienced at this healing was different. His twisted hand and arm began to straighten out. His leg turned around until it was completely normal. His back and neck became straight and within thirty seconds, the crippled man stood before me straight and tall, with both hands, both feet, and his entire body completely normal.

Every eye was on this man. A quietness fell upon the entire auditorium. A miracle healing had taken place that could be measured. The man was complete. His body was shalom.

He looked at me and said, "Thank you." I said, "Don't thank me. Thank the Lord." He looked up and said, "Thank you, Lord," and started walking across the auditorium in front of the long line of people who were waiting for ministry.

The side wall at the university was glass from ceiling to floor. Every eye was still on him as he walked through the glass doors, down the long hallway, and out of the building one hundred percent healed by the power of God. The gift of faith had been distributed to me. I was totally confident that his healing would be complete. What looked impossible an hour earlier became reality within me even before I saw the healing take place.

The gift on the inside changed the circumstances on the outside.

The Blending of the Gifts

I have often been asked what gift of the Spirit was in operation that resulted in the total restoration of the man in Quincy, Illinois. Actually, there were several gifts in operation—the gift of faith, the gifts of healings, the gift of miracles, and the word of wisdom. The gift of faith brought the supernatural belief that this man would be healed. There was no doubt or uncertainty, but a full confidence that was so overpowering that the impending miracle was fully expected. When the miracle took place, there was no amazement because what happened was expected. The only amazement that could have happened would have been had the man not been healed. His physical deliverance was anticipated as sure as the sun would rise in the morning.

Another gift in operation was the gifts of healings. This is obvious because the man was physically healed. But the working of miracles was present and is evident by the immediate manifestation and reconstruction of his body.

Shortly after the meeting, I received a letter from a lady who had also come forward for ministry. She said that she was standing about ten feet from this man when this miracle took place and she described what she saw. But it was very interesting how she described what she heard. While the entirety of the healing only took twenty to thirty seconds, that can seem like a long time when something this powerful happens. I have heard stories about people who were in major accidents and they talked about how their entire lives flashed before them in a moment.

Even though this miraculous event only took half a minute or less, the lady described the sound of his bones snapping back into place as someone slowly breaking a stick of celery. While healing sometimes is a process over a period of time, this instance was a miracle healing that took place over a period of moments.

The fourth gift that was in operation was the word of wisdom. As I stepped in front of this man, I proclaimed to him out of my heart. I spoke by the Holy Spirit and told him that if he could believe that he would be healed, he would be healed. I was proclaiming to him what would take place in the future and giving him the requirement for that event to take place. When he looked at me and confirmed his belief, the supernatural miraculous healing took place.

When natural faith grows by hearing the Word (Romans 10:17), or when the gift of faith is imparted, an act of faith must be done in order to activate the substance of faith and complete the will of the Spirit. Even though the four gifts were imparted, the manifestation of the miracle hinged on the statement by the crippled man when he said, "I believe." Had he not spoken those two words, he would have quenched the moving of the Spirit and he would have left the same way he entered.

Faith is Always Present

You will find every time in the Scriptures when someone was healed or a miracle took place, there was an act of faith. It might have been to stand up and take up their bed, or stretch forth their hand, but some act of faith took place in every instance.

When the supernatural miraculous power of God is in manifestation, faith is always present. Sometimes faith is in the person working the miracle and sometimes faith is in the person receiving the miracle, but regardless, faith must be present.

I have heard it taught that faith must always be in the person receiving the miracle or the healing. But if the person who requires the miracle or healing is either unconscious or dead, it is impossible for them to be acting in faith. When Jesus commanded the body of Lazarus to come forth from the dead, it was obviously not the faith of Lazarus that was in action, but the faith of Jesus. But in other places, faith was present in the person receiving (Mark 5:34; Mark 10:52). Either way, faith is the catalyst that activates the grace that provides what we have hoped for.

Now faith is the substance of things hoped for, the evidence of things not seen.

Hebrews 11:1

CHAPTER 11

THE GIFTS OF HEALINGS
Fourth Gift

But the manifestation of the Spirit is given to each one for the profit of all ... to another gifts of healings by the same Spirit...

1 Corinthians 12:7,9

Definition: These gifts of healings are to deliver the sick and afflicted and to destroy the works of the devil in the human body.

The greatest Healer to ever walk on earth was the Son of God, Jesus. Everywhere He went, He healed all who were sick and oppressed by the devil. Before He ascended, Jesus commissioned all who would believe in Him to heal the sick. One of the gifts He gave through the Holy Spirit is healing of the physical body.

The Parallel Flow

In the course of nature, healing is a process. God created our bodies with a natural system that fights disease. When we have an illness or injury and we are treated by a physician, it usually takes time for the recovery process to fully implement the healing. When a physician administers medication, the person receiving the medication usually does not move from the depths of sickness to total healing in an instant.

While we are thankful for the medical profession and advances in medical science, and while God fully intends for us to use the natural knowledge and wisdom that we have, the healing that comes from God by the way of the Holy Spirit is supernatural and is not restricted to a recovery process. God has provided a gift for the church that can be administered and received several different ways. Each of these ways is a gift of healing and collectively they are the gifts of healings. From the day the church was birthed after Jesus placed His blood on the altar until the time He returns, He has equipped the church with multiple ways to be healed.

Call for the Elders

James, the half brother of Jesus, was the first pastor of the church in Jerusalem. Not only did he verbally teach them as they gathered, but he gave them written instructions on how to conduct themselves. The Book of James in the New Testament is his letter of instruction, not just to the church in Jerusalem, but to all believers.

In his letter he said, *"Is anyone among you sick? Let him call for the elders of the church, and let them pray over him, anointing him with oil in the name of the Lord. And the prayer of faith will save the sick, and the Lord will raise him up"* (James 5:14-15).

James clearly told the Christians in the early church what to do if they were sick. It was the responsibility of the sick person to call for the elders of the church. The elders were to anoint them with oil in the name of the Lord and pray the prayer of faith. By doing this, the sick person would be healed. This was to be done as an act of obedience. This same instruction is for the church today.

This scripture is not talking about the gifts of healings, because the gifts of healings are distributed by the Holy Spirit as He wills. The healing referred to in James' letter is the result of the conscious action of a sick person submitting to the eldership of the church. The responsibility of the prayer of faith is upon the elder. While it is possible that a gift of healing could be distributed to the elder as he prays, according to this scripture, it is not required. This lets us know that while the gifts of healings are important for the supernatural manifestation in the healing of the human body, God has also made provision for all Christians to be healed at any time.

Healings on the Day of Pentecost

The Bible tells of many healings at the hands of Jesus. Although these healings occurred under the Old Covenant, I would like to emphasize that they did not stop when He ascended. Jesus commissioned His followers to continue healing the sick. These healings further prove that supernatural healing from God did not pass away when Jesus departed to heaven, but were to continue in the church until His return.

The Holy Spirit was poured out upon the church on the Day of Pentecost and one of the first demonstrations of power that took place happened as Peter and John went to the temple at 3 o'clock in the afternoon for prayer. As we have detailed earlier, a man who had been lame from birth was immediately healed.

Because many signs and wonders were being done at the hands of the apostles, people were bringing the sick out into the streets and laying them on beds and couches. The anointing upon Peter was so great that as he would pass by, the mere presence of his shadow brought healing (Acts 5:15). Multitudes of people from surrounding cities who heard about what was happening came to Jerusalem and they brought their sick and those who were tormented by unclean spirits. The Scriptures tell us in Acts 5:16 that they were all healed.

Peter, being full of the Holy Spirit, operated in supernatural gifts of healings and although the manifestations may have seemed unusual, the end result was for the benefit of all who were sick. They were healed.

Healing is the Will of God

God wants His people healed. When Jesus was here on earth, the Bible tells us over and over again that He went about teaching the good news and healing all who were sick and afflicted (Matthew 9:35). Jesus believed healing was so important that He even healed on the Sabbath day (Mark 3:1-5). That was against the Jewish custom of the day, but Jesus healed anyway.

Jesus said that He didn't say or do anything unless His Father told Him to. Jesus said in John 12:49-50, *"For I have not spoken on My own authority: but the Father who sent Me gave Me a command, what I should say and what I should speak. And I know that His command is everlasting life. Therefore, whatever I speak, just as the Father has told Me, so I speak."* This clearly shows that healing is the will of the Father also.

Hebrews 13:8 says, *"Jesus Christ is the same yesterday, today and forever."* What does this mean? Well, it means what it says. Jesus has not changed. The things He wanted to accomplish in the past, He wants to accomplish today. If Jesus healed the sick in the past, then He will heal the sick today.

Most Christians believe that God has the power to heal. Most Christians believe that God has healed and occasionally performs miracle healings today from time to time. But some of these same Christians do not believe that healing is for them.

In Mark chapter 6, Jesus went to His hometown of Nazareth. His intentions were to do the same thing there He did everywhere else. Everywhere He went He preached the gospel. Everywhere He went He preached the good news of the kingdom. Everywhere He went He healed the sick. But at Nazareth, however, He was unable to do any great miracles. Why? Well let's look at the Bible, the Word of God, and see why.

In Mark 6:5-6 it says, *"Now He could do no mighty work there, except that He laid His hands on a few sick people and healed them. And He marveled because of their unbelief."*

Belief is essential in healing, and that's where Satan attacks. If Satan can get us to doubt that healing is for us, then healing will be difficult. Satan's will for you is sickness, disease, and death. Satan's will for your life is totally opposite to the will of God for you. *"The thief does not come except to steal, and to kill, and to destroy. I have come that they may have life, and that they may have it more abundantly"* (John 10:10).

Sadly, some Christians believe that healing does exist, but they don't truly believe it can happen to them.

If we don't believe that we can be healed, we will be like the people of Nazareth. They didn't believe, so they didn't receive. If you have sickness in your body, then I encourage you to believe that Jesus not only can heal, but that He will heal you. God's will is that you be healed.

Jesus said to him, "If you can believe, all things are possible to him who believes."

Mark 9:23

Let me ask you this. Is it possible that you could wake up tomorrow and the illness or sickness that has afflicted you for years would be gone? Is it possible that the disease that has come upon you and drained your finances could be completely eliminated? Well, the answer is yes. Is it possible for everybody? No! It's not for everybody. It's only for those who believe.

Knot on the Neck

Back in the early days of my ministry, I was asked to speak at an evangelical church in downtown Kansas City. As I walked to the platform to speak that Sunday morning, the Holy Spirit guided me to teach on healing. When I gave an altar call for healing, it appeared that the entire church came forward. In fact, a line formed that went down the side of the church all the way to the back and around the pews at the far end of the church. One by one I laid hands on the people and proclaimed healing. Like people waiting to enter an event, after I finished laying hands on one individual, the next person would step in front of me, I would pray for them, and then they would go and take their seat in the church.

After I was about halfway through the line, a very large lady moved into position for prayer. When I asked her what she wanted to receive from the Lord, she pointed to her neck where there was a knot below her ear about the size of a golf ball. She began to tell her story. She said that she noticed this knot about six months earlier and she came to church for healing. The minister prayed with her and she went home. Her husband, who did not attend church anywhere and was a nonbeliever, ridiculed her and told her that if God was real, the knot would have been healed.

She said over the next six months she attended several meetings at the church where there were several guest speakers. Every time there was an altar call, she went forward for healing, and every trip home brought more ridicule from her unbelieving husband. Instead of the knot decreasing in size, she said it increased in size and once again pointing at her neck, she said, "You can see how large it is now."

Then she told me that she had gone to the doctor and the doctor said it really wasn't any major problem, but that they could easily remove this large knot from her neck. She was scheduled to go to the hospital the very next day and have it surgically removed. So her prayer request was not necessarily for healing, but that her unbelieving husband would realize that God can also work through doctors, and that he would no longer ridicule her, but believe.

Upon hearing this, I laid hands on her and proclaimed that she was healed. I told her to lift her hands and thank God for her healing. Her eyes were closed and she was definitely feeling the power of the Spirit of God. When I spoke to her and said, "Believe that you are healed," she said in a calm voice, "I am healed."

She took her right hand down from above her head and reached across her body to touch the knot below her ear on the left side of her neck. When she did that, she made a startling discovery. The knot was gone completely and her neck was normal. She was so shocked that she thought she had touched the wrong side of her neck and immediately pulled down her left hand and reached below her ear on the right side. For the next few seconds, she was grabbing both sides of her neck with opposite hands. And then this lady began to dance and scream!

After a few moments of dancing, she took off running. She ran across the front of the church to the opposite side of where the line was coming forward. She ran down the side of the church and grabbing a pew with her right hand, swung around the back of the church and started running across the back.

The senior pastor had been casually standing near the back while I had been praying for the people at the front. I will never forget the look on his face when he glanced up and saw this lady barreling toward him with arms and legs flailing in all directions. She had been healed and her joy could not be restrained! Needless to say, her husband became a believer and the last I heard was still regularly attending church with her.

A Knot in St. Louis

It was during those years of ministry that almost every week I was speaking and giving my testimony at a Full Gospel Businessman's Fellowship International meeting. In those days they would advertise me as the former Southern Baptist pastor who had been filled with the Holy Spirit. As I traveled to these meetings, the testimony of the lady with the knot on her neck was one of my stories.

After speaking at a Full Gospel Businessman's meeting in St. Louis, Missouri, a man came forward and said, "I am just like the lady you prayed for in Kansas City." He showed me a knot on the left side of his neck below his ear that was the size of a golf ball. He then told me that it had increased over six months and that he also was going in to have it surgically removed that very week. He told me he had been prayed for several times and that he was very impressed with my story of the lady in Kansas City. He knew this was his night—his miracle was here. He threw his hands into the air and he said, "I receive."

I laid hands on him and proclaimed the same healing over him that I had proclaimed over the lady in Kansas City and

145

when I said, "Believe that you are healed," he brought down his right hand and reached across to his neck. But unlike the lady in Kansas City, his knot was still there. I was positive that it would be gone, but it was not. I encouraged the man and headed back home to the Lake of the Ozarks.

A friend of mine, who was a good Christian and a local businessman, had driven me to the meeting in St. Louis knowing that it would be a very late night and a long drive home for me. On the way home, he asked me the question, "Why would God heal the lady in Kansas City and not heal the man in St. Louis?" That night I didn't have an answer.

The Answer

After about six months, I had a meeting scheduled at a large resort hotel at the Lake of the Ozarks with nationally-known speakers. One evening before the meeting there was a large banquet where people sat at round tables with a catered meal and elegant surroundings. While Loretta and I were walking past one of the tables, a man looked up and spoke to me by saying, "Remember me?" While he looked vaguely familiar, he could tell by the look on my face that I didn't know who he was. He said, "You remember that night in St. Louis when you prayed for the knot on my neck, and after you prayed it was still there." I thought to myself, "Thanks for reminding me!" Then he said, "Look, it's gone!" and proceeded to tell me the story.

He said that night after I had prayed for him, he went home and told his wife what had happened. They decided to postpone his surgery for a week. After a week, the knot appeared to be slightly smaller, so they postponed his surgery for a couple more weeks. After two more weeks, it was definitely decreasing in size and as long as it decreased, they postponed his surgery until a point was reached where surgery was not needed. The doctor certified that there was no trace of a knot ever having been there. While he was telling me this story, his wife who was seated next to him, kept saying, "That's right. He's telling the truth! This is exactly how it happened!" After giving me a big hug, I continued on with my duties of the evening.

That night God taught me a great spiritual truth. Healing is a process that takes time, but a miracle healing takes place in a moment of time. While the lady in Kansas City experienced the gift of healing and the gift of miracles by the Holy Spirit, the man in St. Louis experienced the gift of healing. While the end result was the same, the distribution of the gifts was at the discretion of the Holy Spirit and not the minister. There are diversities of activities, administration, and timing, but the ultimate result is deliverance and victory.

While many people desire healing, in their mind they are actually thinking miracle healing. But it is the Holy Spirit who distributes the gift and it is always for the benefit of all. It was also confirmed to me that there are various administrations and manifestations and blendings of the gifts. We should never predetermine how God is going to do something, but in faith continue to believe and receive His goodness.

Don't Stop Believing

While ministering at a men's prayer breakfast in a small rural town in northern Missouri, the man who invited me to speak asked if I would pray for the men as they left the meeting. While praying for a middle aged farmer in bib overalls, I noticed a growth on his face about two inches below his eye. It looked like a wart except that it was about the size of a quarter. When I asked him about it, he replied that his doctor thought it was cancerous and they were going to remove it in a few weeks.

I prayed with him and as he turned and walked toward the door to leave the small dining room area in the restaurant, I heard the Spirit of God tell me to tell him to stop, so I immediately called for him to stop. He turned and looked toward me and I only spoke what I heard the Spirit of God saying through me. I pointed at the growth on the man's face from about ten feet away and I boldly said, "Be cursed, in the name of Jesus!" Although it may have looked like I was cursing the man to the people in the room, I still had to say what I heard the Spirit say. The man looked at me and acknowledged he understood the statement by nodding his head, and then left the building.

Several years passed and I heard nothing from this man until one day he stopped by our ministry office as he was traveling through the Lake of the Ozarks. He spoke to the receptionist to give me a message. He said, "Tell Brother Ollison that just a few days after he pointed his finger at the growth on my face and cursed it, something miraculous happened. I was shaving early in the morning and as I was cleaning my razor, I heard something clink in the sink where I was shaving. I looked down and the growth that had been on my face—that ugly, hard piece of flesh—had fallen off. I went to the doctor to be examined and he said, "Except for the fact that there is no suntan where the growth was, it appears that there never has been one."

When I received that message from the receptionist at my office, my heart leaped for joy as I learned one more truth. When the Holy Spirit speaks, we must say what He says and when He says without delay.

Postponed obedience is disobedience. If we speak what the Spirit speaks, then our words will be like the words of Jesus. Jesus said, *"The words that I speak to you are spirit, and they are life"* (John 6:63). If we want to experience the same miraculous power in our lives that Jesus experienced in His, and if we want His prophetic words to come to pass where He said, "The same works that I do will those do who believe in Me" (John 14:12), then we must speak the words of the Spirit in the same way He spoke the words of the Spirit. When we do this, our words will be spirit and they will be life to all who hear them.

Seeking God's Guidance for Healing

When my son was a newborn, he could not keep milk down. Whatever went in his mouth just came right back up. Instead of gaining weight, he was losing weight.

One day I was at the boat marina when Loretta called me and said she had taken Robbie to the local doctor. The doctor had told her Robbie had pyloric stenosis, which is a tightening of the muscle at the bottom of the stomach so that food cannot get from the stomach to the intestines. Robbie had lost so much weight that the doctor believed if they didn't get him into surgery immediately, he would die. This doctor wanted to fly him by helicopter to Columbia for surgery that very day.

The first thing we did was to seek God's wisdom. We immediately prayed together on the phone and after prayer decided we would follow peace. In our hearts it seemed right that we should quickly get a second opinion. We got in touch with Dr. Glaspy in Clinton, Missouri, who was the doctor who had delivered Robbie. In talking with him, he told us about a new miracle drug that had just come out. He said for years the only treatment for pyloric stenosis was to operate on babies by cutting them open and cutting the muscle at the bottom of the stomach. He told us they could get the drug that same day and if we started Robbie on it, he wouldn't have to have surgery.

We prayed and God guided us to start the medicine that day. It began to loosen up the muscles and he gradually started getting better, and he didn't have to go through surgery.

That was a healing, but there was also wisdom in that. We had to hear from God and do what He said. We could have flown him to Columbia for the surgery and he probably would have recovered, but then he would have had a scar for the rest of his life.

The doctor who suggested the surgery told Loretta that even if our son survived the pyloric stenosis, he would always be puny. Looking back, that seems quite humorous now because in high school, our son was 6'4" and the captain of two state championship football teams.

When healing is needed, we must always seek the wisdom of God first and by His Spirit, He will speak to us.

All Knowledge Comes from God

All the knowledge and wisdom of the medical profession has been given by God by revelation of the Holy Spirit. Throughout history, many plagues and catastrophic diseases that affected millions have been averted because of a miracle vaccine that was revealed by inspiration of the Holy Spirit.

Knowledge is good. It's much better to have an understanding of how something works than to be unknowledgeable. In an office setting, when a mechanical device breaks, we call a technician to repair it. Why? Because the technician knows how the broken devise works. Through his training, knowledge, and understanding he can repair it.

While it is good to have knowledge of natural things and to understand them, sometimes this can be a hindrance when it comes to healing. Because we understand the cause of a sickness, the current methods of treatment, and the probable outcome, the tendency is to think in the realm of the natural and exclude a spiritual solution. Sometimes when it comes to sickness, we just know too much.

While it may be wisdom to research a diagnosis for the understanding of treatment, to continually dwell on the negative outcome and do never-ending searches for information can hinder your faith and therefore, block your healing.

Regardless of our knowledge of a medical condition, we must submit ourselves to the spiritual truths of God and allow Him to heal us through His Holy Spirit. This does not mean that we do not go to doctors, nor does it mean that we do not seek a medical cure.

While we do not discredit or exclude the medical profession, but are thankful for the knowledge and wisdom they do have, we cannot allow this understanding to keep us from seeking what God wants to do physically in our bodies. Let's put it this way. Because of increased medical understanding, many seek natural medical healing first and if that fails, then they turn to God. However, the biblical principle is that we are to seek God first in everything. Spiritual healing should not be the last resort, but instead should be the first option. Instead of taking an aspirin for a headache, pray first.

But seek first the kingdom of God and His righteousness, and all these things shall be added to you.
Matthew 6:33

Expect the Unexpected

A businessman in Columbia, Missouri, asked me to speak to some of his associates at a luncheon. Upon arriving and entering the lunch room, I could see that there were going to be around 30 to 40 business people in attendance. After glancing around the room, the gentleman who had invited me took me by the arm and said, "There is an elderly gentleman who attends these luncheons who has a severe hearing problem and he usually turns off his hearing aids and sleeps. The reason I am telling you is because he snores loudly and I wanted you to know that could happen while you are talking." I smiled and assured him that would not bother me. As a public speaker, you learn to handle distractions that come in many different ways.

At the luncheon I shared about the power of agreement in prayer from Matthew 18:19 and I gave a couple of illustrations of how God took something that seemed impossible and made it a reality. I could tell that all through the meeting the elderly gentleman with the hearing loss stayed awake and kept his eyes fixed on me. When the meeting was over, he approached me and I asked him what I could do for him. In an extremely loud voice he shouted, "I want to hear." All I did was place my hand on his head and in a normal voice I said, "In the name of Jesus be healed."

Immediately the man's eyes opened wide and he took a step back as he yanked the hearing aids out of his ears. He said, "Why are you yelling at me?" When we finally figured out what was going on, we both laughed. It was humorous! When he came forward for prayer, his hearing was so poor that his hearing aids were turned up to the maximum setting. At the moment he became healed, the sound coming from the hearing aids was unbearable.

It's interesting that this meeting was not a church meeting; it was a luncheon. The elderly man, who was a business owner in town, attended the luncheon out of a sense of obligation and had no thought that it was the day his hearing would be totally healed. All it took was the laying on of hands and receiving, and of course, the Holy Spirit imparting the gift of healing and the working of miracles.

When this gentleman woke up that morning, he had no idea that when he went to bed that night he would no longer need hearing aids constantly cranked to the highest setting, but would have normal hearing.

God has a plan for your deliverance. Always be ready for the Holy Spirit to move in your life. Be led by the Spirit and expect the unexpected.

The Blind Lady

As I have traveled over the years, there are some meetings that are more memorable than others and, of course, these are the meetings where you actually see the power of the Holy Spirit miraculously change lives. While ministering at one of these life-changing meetings, I saw some of the greatest physical miracles I have ever seen in my life.

Later, as the meeting was drawing to a close and people were standing amazed at the miracles that had taken place, an elderly blind lady made her way to the front. She was using a white cane that she moved from side to side and there was a middle-aged man with her.

Because of a powerful healing miracle that had just occurred, I anticipated this lady's miraculous healing also. I laid hands on her and proclaimed her healing. As I stood back, I could see no change. She nodded a thank you and with her white cane and the middle-aged man helping her, she made her way toward the exit and left the building. Although I had just witnessed a miracle so great that it changed the course of my ministry, I was puzzled and wondered why the blind lady wasn't healed.

Approximately twenty years passed and we received a letter at the church. It was written by the son of the blind lady who was the middle-aged man helping her the night of the meeting. In his letter he said, "You may not remember my mother, but years ago she was at a meeting," and he described the town and place. He said, "She came forward for healing because she was blind." Of course, I remembered that meeting. It had always been a mystery to me concerning the blind lady.

The letter continued. "It had been raining that night before the meeting and as we walked out of the building to the parking lot, the parking lot was still wet. My wife waited with my mom at the curb as I went to get the car. We always did this so that mom would not have to walk any great distances because of her blindness. As I approached the car, I heard my wife and mother screaming from the curb. Running back to them, I heard my mother shouting, 'I can see! I can see!' We were so excited we got in the car and went home.

"My mother had not driven an automobile for years, but immediately started driving again. She passed her driving and eye exam without any problems. She even went to WalMart to get glasses because all of her friends had glasses. She thought perhaps she would need glasses, but upon examining her, they found she had perfect eyesight. Glasses were not needed.

"The reason I am writing you is because mom recently passed away and on the day she moved to heaven, she had perfect eyesight. My wife and I realized that we never went back into the meeting to tell you what had happened. So we decided to write."

Don't Give Up on Your Healing

Because of his letter, I experienced great joy, but it also reinforced a spiritual truth. The miracle power of God operates in the timing of the Spirit and not the natural timing of man. Even when we don't see an immediate manifestation of our miracle, that doesn't mean that it's not in the womb waiting to be birthed.

Too often when we ask for something from God, if we don't see it within moments of saying amen, we lose faith and by losing faith, we lose the miracle. When Jesus cursed the fig tree, it immediately died at the roots, but the disciples did not notice that it had withered until the next day (Mark 11:20-21). When we need something accomplished in the realm of the physical, it first happens in the realm of the unseen, and our faith brings it back into the physical realm.

There are scriptures that talk about how some were healed within the hour, while others were healed as they went, and others were healed immediately. The end result was the same for all of them. They were healed. Do not allow what you see to affect your faith.

For we walk by faith, not by sight.

2 Corinthians 5:7

CHAPTER 12

THE GIFT OF THE WORKING OF MIRACLES
Fifth Gift

But the manifestation of the Spirit is given to each
one for the profit of all ... to another the working of
miracles ...

1 Corinthians 12:7,10

Definition: The gift of the working of miracles is the supernatural suspension of the course of nature and physics to manifest the impossible in the realm of the physical through the Spirit of God.

I looked at the writings of three great men of God who have passed on to see how they described the gift of the working of miracles.

Kenneth E. Hagin said, "A miracle is a supernatural intervention into the ordinary course of nature. It's a temporary suspension of the accustomed order through the Spirit of God."[1]

---

1 Kenneth E. Hagin, *The Holy Spirit and His Gifts*, (Tulsa: Rhema Bible Church, 1991), 126.

Lester Sumrall said, "In the gift of the working of miracles, God is entrusting us with a strength, with an energy that we do not normally have. It is the power of the Spirit of God surging through us, through our hands, our feet, our minds, causing us to do something that is not normal or natural to our behavior."[2]

Howard Carter said this. "We might say that it is the supernatural demonstration of the power of God by which the laws of nature are altered, suspended, or controlled."[3]

The Power Behind a Miracle

Sometimes the world will use the word *miracle* and cheapen it. For example, I've seen commercials advertising a "miracle fabric," or a "miracle mop," or "miracle detergent." While these items might be new to the marketplace and while it may add a new dimension to the product, it only diminishes the depth of what a miracle actually is in the minds of men. And the natural use of the word *miracle* does not even slightly compare to the depth and fullness of the word when used in the Scripture.

In the Bible, a miracle is an instantaneous and divine energizing of power. In the church, the gift of the working of miracles enables a believer to accomplish something through the Spirit which, according to the laws of nature and physics, is impossible.

---

2 Lester Sumrall, *The Gifts and Ministries of the Holy Spirit*, (New Kensington: Whitaker House, 1982), 105.
3 Howard Carter, *Questions & Answers On Spiritual Gifts*, (Tulsa: Harrison House, Inc., 1976), 82.

I found it interesting when I started doing a word study on the "working of miracles," that the Greek word for "working" is *energēmata* which is where we get the English word "energy." The English word for "of miracles" is the Greek word *dynameōn*. This is the same root word Jesus used in Acts 1:8 where He said that the new believers would receive power (*dynamin*) when the Holy Spirit would come upon them.

These two references solidify this truth: The Holy Spirit is the miracle working power of God on earth.

The Parallel Flow

When we talk about the gifts of the Spirit, with many of the gifts there is a natural flow and the supernatural flow. When it comes to miracles, there are miracles that take place in your life because you pray in faith, ask, and receive.

Years ago, I knew a man who was living an ordinary life. His parents owned a business that had gone bankrupt decades before. When his parents died, this man received no inheritance because of the bankruptcy.

One day he went to the mailbox and found an envelope that contained a check for $125,000. It was totally unexpected, but through a bankruptcy settlement, he received an inheritance check. He had no knowledge that the check existed or was even in the process of settlement before that day.

You may feel you have no resources, but God has resources that you know nothing about. This man had been praying in faith, asking, and believing God for financial deliverance. God can give you a miraculous deliverance like He did this man. You may not see the possibility of a miracle, but God can make a way when it appears there is no way. He can open a door when you can't even find the door. He has hidden miracles that He can reveal through His Spirit.

While this man's deliverance was joyfully received, it occurred through what appeared to be a natural process. However, there are times in our lives when we need an immediate, supernatural miracle that goes beyond logic and the natural laws of nature and physics. This is when we need the supernatural deliverance that is only available through the Holy Spirit.

There is a power that is available to Christians that is distributed by God as He wills. This power is outside the normal course of nature. It is the gift of the working of miracles.

Miraculous Deliverance

While the early church was going through great persecution, King Herod was harassing the church. He killed James, the brother of John, with the sword. After he did this, he saw that it pleased the unbelieving Jews, so he arrested Peter during the Days of Unleavened Bread. Upon his arrest, he was placed in prison and four squads of soldiers were assigned to guard him. Herod's intention was to bring Peter before the people after Passover.

The night before Herod was going to present Peter to the public for ridicule and execution, Peter was sleeping in prison. Because he was such a high profile prisoner, he was bound with two chains between two soldiers and there were additional guards by the door of the prison. But while he was in prison, the church was praying.

During the night, an angel of the Lord stood by him and a light shone in the prison. The angel of the Lord struck Peter on the side and raised him up and said, *"Arise quickly."* When the angel spoke these words, the chains fell off of Peter's hands. Then the angel told him to get dressed and put on his sandals. After Peter did this, he was further instructed to put on his outer garment and to follow the angel. As the angel moved to exit the prison, Peter followed him.

What was happening was so surreal that Peter thought to himself that it was possibly a vision. They went past the first guard post, past the second guard post, and they came to the huge iron gate that leads to the city. Gates of this type usually would require several soldiers to open it because of its size, but the gate opened by itself without any physical assistance. The angel led Peter out of the prison and down the street, and then the angel departed. (Acts 12:1-10.)

In this account of Peter in prison, we see several miracles and some hidden truths about the working of miracles. First, we must recognize that the reason Peter was in prison was because of his bold stand in proclaiming that Jesus was the Christ. He was not in prison because he robbed a liquor store! We also can note that Peter was not worried or complaining to God about his situation. In fact, on the eve of his probable execution he was sleeping.

As his release was taking place, there were some things that took place miraculously and some things that took place naturally. At least two things happened miraculously: the chains fell off of his wrists and the huge iron gate opened of its own accord. But there were things Peter was told to do. He was told to put on his own shoes and undergarments, to put on his outer garment, and to walk behind the angel out of the prison.

At one time early in my ministry, I asked the Lord this question. If He removed the chains and opened the gate, why did He make Peter tie his own sandals and put on his own clothes? The answer was quite simple. God miraculously did what Peter couldn't do, but required him to do what he could do. While Peter could not remove the chains and open the gate, he certainly could tie his own shoes.

We must always remember that while the miracle power of God is for the church, we must not expect God to do what He has told us to do.

The Faith of a Child for a Miracle

When my son, Robbie, was a little tyke, he rode his bicycle off the roof of a boat storage building. (I didn't ask then, and I still don't want to know how or why he did it!) We immediately took him to the emergency room at the local clinic.

Dr. Lyle showed us the x-ray of the broken bone in his wrist. He told us that this particular bone was important to the mobility of his hand and if it didn't heal right, it would actually affect his hand's normal growth. To make sure the bone was properly set, he required us to come back the next week to have it x-rayed again. The cast went from his elbow to his fingers.

On our way home that day, Robbie told us that he had heard from the Spirit of God and that his wrist was completely healed. Well, you know how parents can be. I kind of had the attitude of "that's cute." Sometimes God can speak to children easier than He can adults because their hearts are so innocent and pure. Robbie said he was healed. He also said, "I'm going to wear this cast anyway, but I know I'm healed."

The next week we took him back to Dr. Lyle. I will never forget when Dr. Lyle came out and told us they had x-rayed Robbie's arm. He said, "His arm is not healed. It's never been broken." I said, "So you mean it is set right?" He said, "No, no. If a bone has been broken and it has grown back together, you can always tell where it was broken. But this bone has never been broken." He said, "I don't get it, so I'm still going to make him wear the cast."

So Robbie wore the cast. But God worked a miracle that day through the faith of a child.

Collateral Glory

Because of the incident in Acts chapter 16 concerning the demon-possessed, fortune-telling girl, the people were extremely angry with Paul and Silas. They were arrested and the rulers stripped them and commanded that they be beaten with rods. After they were severely beaten, they were thrown into prison and the jailer was given the command to keep them secure. After hearing this, he put them into the inner prison and fastened their feet in stocks. (Acts 16:22-24.)

This command to the jailer was not taken lightly. According to Roman military regulations, if someone escaped from prison, the guard on watch received their punishment. If someone was scheduled to be crucified the next day and they escaped, the guard who was in charge of them would be crucified instead, so they were very intent on keeping people in jail.

At midnight, Paul and Silas were praying and singing hymns to God and the prisoners were listening to them. They had a captive audience. Suddenly there was an earthquake and the foundations of the prison shook. Immediately all the prison doors opened and everyone's chains fell off.

The shaking of the foundations woke up the keeper of the prison and when he saw that the prison doors were open, he assumed the prisoners had escaped. He drew his sword and was getting ready to kill himself when Paul called out with a loud voice saying, *"Do yourself no harm, for we are all here."* The jailer called for a light, ran into the prison cell, and fell down before Paul and Silas. He was trembling. Then he brought them out of the prison and said, *"Sirs, what must I do to be saved?"* (Acts 16:25-30).

The rest of the story is the keeper of the prison got saved, his family got saved, they all got baptized that night, and there was a great revival as a result of this miracle. When this miracle took place, it wasn't just about Paul and Silas. It was about all the collateral glory that came with it. People's lives were changed.

Believe for the Impossible

As Christians, we should believe for the impossible, but not just for the impossible to happen to us, but believe that the gift of working of miracles will be bestowed upon us so that through us everyone can benefit.

When a miracle happens in your life, your countenance and your attitude will automatically change and others will notice. The change in your life will affect other lives. Not only was Paul delivered, but also the jailer. Deliverance can be contagious and go viral and other lives will be changed.

Why do you think the Bible tells us twelve men—just normal guys, and some just fisherman—turned the world upside down for Jesus? (Acts 17:6). How did they do it? It wasn't because of their eloquent speaking. It was the miracle power! Paul said, "My speech was not with persuasive words, but in demonstration of the Spirit and of power!" (1 Corinthians 2:4).

The Bible says that Paul, the apostle, performed unusual miracles (Acts 19:11). There were times his handkerchief would be passed around and when people touched it, they were instantly healed (Acts 19:12). Also, it is recorded that the shadow of Peter would bring healing to the sick (Acts 5:15-16).

Go beyond believing for the normal. Miracles by their very nature are unusual and appear impossible. To receive the impossible, you must believe for the impossible.

The working of miracles can work through you also. This gift is received the same way the other gifts of the Spirit are received. You desire the gift, you believe for the gift, and when it is imparted, you receive the gift.

While we know that it is the Holy Spirit who distributes the gifts at His will, we must also know and understand that

He is looking for a willing vessel who by faith is believing to receive.

A Very Strange and Unusual Miracle

Jesus operated in miracles and He said, "The same things that I am doing now, you will do" (John 14:12). Here Jesus proclaimed that He was a worker of miracles and prophesied that in the future, miracles would take place at the hands of His followers.

One day while the disciples were in Capernaum, the people who received the temple tax asked Peter if his Teacher was going to pay the temple tax. Peter told them, "Yes." Before Peter had a chance to ask Jesus about it, Jesus told Peter what to do.

He said, "You're a fisherman, right? Go fishing and the first fish you catch, instead of just throwing it up on the bank, look in its mouth and you will find a piece of money." (Matthew 17:24-27.)

Peter had a choice. He could either believe the bizarre story Jesus told him about money being in the mouth of the fish, or he could reject it. His choice would determine whether or not his taxes would get paid. To reject and not believe Jesus would require no action—just simply walk away and do nothing. To believe what Jesus said required an act of faith.

First of all, he had to throw in a hook and when he caught the first fish, he had to look in its mouth for the coin. I've always wondered if he looked around to see if anybody was watching. It had to look strange! When he believed and followed the words of Jesus, a miracle occurred and there was enough money in the mouth of the fish to pay the temple tax for Peter and for Jesus.

Remember, Jesus said that the same things that occurred miraculously in His ministry would occur in the ministry of those who follow Him. Increase your faith, believe for the miraculous, and receive unusual and unconventional deliverance.

Snow Storm Miracle

Late one October, my wife and I were scheduled to attend a ministers' conference in Colorado Springs, Colorado. Another couple in our church, who were newlyweds and making this conference their honeymoon, decided they would follow us as they had experienced mechanical issues with their automobile and wanted to stay close.

The weather was unpredictable this time of the year and the forecast was for the possibility of snow. This was not unusual and since most of the trip was to take place on Interstate 70, we anticipated no problems. As we traveled from Central Missouri through Kansas City and into Kansas, we began to hear reports of a severe snowstorm that could possibly be heading across the western half of Kansas. As we heard the weather reports, the couple behind us called and asked if we should turn around and head back.

But there were several things we knew. First, we knew we were to be in Colorado Springs at this conference. We knew if God wanted us there, He would get us there, and we knew we had authority over the weather.

It takes several hours to cross the state of Kansas, and as we continued on, we heard on the radio that the storm had increased and that portions of I-70 had been closed due to the snow accumulating so rapidly that the snow plows had not been able to clear the roads. Although we had not seen any snow yet, not even any flurries, the radio announcer kept talking about the denseness of the storm. It was almost as though the radio was reporting from somewhere else. Just as we were hearing that the interstate was closed all the way to Colorado, traffic in the west bound lane began to slow and both lanes headed west came to a stop.

I was wondering why the traffic had stopped, because no snow could be seen. Although it was overcast and it looked snowy, there was no snow. We had been reading Charles Capps' book on angels and confessing that the angels would clear a path for us, and we had been taking authority over the storm, but the forecast sounded devastating.

About a mile ahead, the highway patrol had blocked the interstate and all cars were being merged into the right lane and onto the off ramp. It took almost 30 minutes until it was our turn to exit at the ramp. The ramp actually was an uphill ramp that led to a road that crossed over the interstate.

At the end of the exit ramp there were two highway patrol cars about ten feet apart with two highway patrolmen standing between them to block anyone from re-entering the ramp on the other side that went back on the interstate. Most of the vehicles on the road were transport trucks and as each vehicle reached the top of the exit ramp, the patrolman would look at them and give them the option of turning right (north) or left (south). The ones turning south could then re-enter the interstate going the opposite direction and head back east away from the devastating blizzard that had blocked the interstate all the way to Colorado.

As we were on the ramp headed to the top, our friends called and asked, "What are we going to do?" My reply was, "Just follow me." I think he was wanting to know if we were going to turn right and try to find another road to Colorado or if we were going to turn left and head back home.

As the car in front of us turned left, the two highway patrolmen looked at me, and to my amazement, instead of motioning us to the left or the right, they each backed away and stood in front of their cars and motioned to me to get on the entry ramp on the other side and continue on the interstate. So I did. I looked in my rear view mirror and they likewise motioned the car behind me to continue. The patrolmen then stepped back between the cars and continued to direct cars to the left and to the right.

We still had several hours of travel before we reached the hotel in Colorado Springs. We drove the speed limit the entire way and the only cars traveling west or east were our two cars. The report on the radio was correct. The interstate was closed. But we never saw any snow the entire trip. Nothing in the sky, nothing on the ground, just overcast and dry roads.

The attendance at the convention was down. Many people had called in and canceled because of the severe weather report. Some had even started driving to the conference, but turned around and went home because the weather was so bad. I have no explanation for why I saw the highway patrolmen turn away hundreds of cars and trucks, but they motioned us back on the interstate and then blocked every vehicle behind us—other than it being a supernatural miracle at the hand of God.

The radio kept reporting that the interstate was blocked by snow and it was impassable. But we saw no snow. The angels of God must have cleared a path for us, just as we confessed.

The Purpose for the Miracle

When I have shared about this miracle publicly, there have been those who have said, "I don't understand how this could happen." That's the way the miracles of God are. They are not understandable by human standards. I'm quite sure it wasn't understandable as the servants were pouring wine out of the water containers they had just filled with water at the marriage feast in Cana. (John 2:1-10.)

Peter's friends must have thought to themselves, "I don't understand this," as he told them how the chains just fell off of his hands while he was in prison and how the huge gate that normally took many men to open, opened by itself so he could walk through. (Acts 2:1-10.)

I'm sure that people watching the disciples feed 5,000 men and their families out of a basket that only contained a few fish and some pieces of bread didn't understand how it could happen. (Matthew 14:13-21.) Once again, the mind of man cannot comprehend the miracle power of God.

At the minister's conference as I would talk with people at lunch, dinner, and social times, I could not find anyone else that had arrived at the conference by way of I-70. Many questions came to mind. "Did it snow but I did not see the snow, or did it not snow but the snow showed up on the weather radar? Why did the highway patrolmen, without words being uttered, motion me back on the interstate but block everyone else? Why did the people reporting the weather say there was a blizzard with the snow so high it was impassable, while we did not see a snowflake?"

To this day, I do not know the answers to these questions and I am thankful that I had a man and a woman in a car behind me from my church to confirm the entire event. But this much I do know. From the beginning I knew that God wanted me there for a purpose and at that meeting even though attendance was low, I had divine appointments that had a lifelong impact on my ministry.

Miracles, by definition, are events that occur outside the normal course of nature and cannot be understood by natural thought. So when a miracle takes place, praise God and thank Him for it, believe it and receive it, and continue with joy.

Teleported to Kansas City

Years ago, Loretta's brother was in the hospital in Independence, Missouri. Earlier in the day he had abdominal surgery where a large mass had been removed. At that time in our lives, Loretta and I were living in Sunrise Beach, Missouri which was about two and a half to three hours away from the hospital where her brother's surgery had taken place.

From the time I was in high school, my family has always been in the marine business with boat dealerships that included a marina on the water, boat storage, and a sales showroom. On that particular day, I had agreed that I would close the business after the employees left, lock it up, and set the alarms. The visiting hours at the hospital started at 7:00 p.m. and lasted until 8:30 so we knew that if I locked the store at 5:00, we could get in our Oldsmobile Trofeo and make it to the hospital for the last thirty minutes of visitation.

The sales people, the office employees, and the technicians clocked out at 5:00 sharp. My father once told me that if you did not believe that the dead can come back to life, then you should stand beside the time clock at quitting time. So with all of the employees timed out and gone, we were getting ready to close the showroom door when an elderly gentleman and his wife walked through.

They were insistent on looking at a boat they wanted to purchase and they asked questions—a lot of questions. It seemed as though they walked slow and talked slow. Even though I told them we needed to leave to see a family member in the hospital, it didn't seem to phase them. When they didn't like certain features on the boat they were looking at, they asked to see some others. Time was slipping away and it seemed like there was no way we would make it to Independence that evening in time to see Loretta's brother.

When the couple finally left and the door was locked and the alarm set, Loretta and I stood in the parking lot and made a decision. Her brother underwent major surgery and we needed to pray for him. Although we could not make it during hospital visiting hours, we knew we could probably get there between nine and 9:30. Because I was a licensed minister, I would see if I could talk the nurse into allowing me in after our long drive.

The first half of the trip seemed to go as normal until we reached the town of Sedalia, Missouri and turned onto US Highway 50. It was a four lane road similar to an interstate and there should have been no problem at all, except that the car in front of us was driving very slowly.

It was going about 5—10 miles an hour below the speed limit—slow enough that I wanted to pass it. But as I would move into the left lane to go around it, it would move into the left lane in front of me. I would drive two or three miles behind the car and then as I would slowly move to the right lane, the car in front of me would also move to the right lane. This went on for approximately 25-50 miles.

Loretta looked at me and said, "Consider it all joy. This must be our angel guiding us to the hospital." We were so late now, it was ridiculous, so we just traveled at normal speed and rejoiced in the Lord all the way to the hospital.

I don't know why we did not check the time. Maybe it was because we knew we were so late that checking the time would only discourage us. But nevertheless, we never looked at our watches.

Upon arriving at the hospital, the parking lot was empty. I quickly got out of my car and, without waiting for Loretta, ran to the door and went inside. A nurse was stationed outside the hallway to the surgery recovery wing of the hospital and there was a waiting room nearby.

The first thing I did was tell her that I was a minister and that we had traveled a great distance to see my wife's brother who had surgery earlier that day. Because of unforeseeable delays I was curious if we would be able to go in now and see him. I told her we wouldn't take long and if he was asleep, we wouldn't wake him. But before we left for our journey back to the Lake of the Ozarks, we were asking if we could just go in for a few moments and pray with him.

I delivered my speech with all the compassion I could and the nurse appeared to be compassionate also in her listening. But when I asked her, she abruptly said, "No, you cannot go in now." I asked her why. She said, "You'll have to wait until the 7:00 pm visiting hour starts, like everyone else." I then looked at the clock on the wall and it was ten minutes before 7:00 pm.

We had not crossed any time zones, and daylight saving time had not started, but somehow we had made a three hour drive in less than an hour. We were delayed at the family business until after 6:00 pm, we traveled behind a slow car that we couldn't seem to get around, and we still traveled approximately 150 miles in less than an hour. By the current driving laws and highway speeds, that is impossible!

So what's the point? This was not something that we asked for. We were on a mission to pray for someone and that was our only goal. Even in the middle of frustrating circumstances, neither one of us allowed the frustration to take the joy from our hearts or derail us from the mission we felt called to. Even though there was a strong possibility we would not be allowed to see her brother, we stepped out in faith and went anyway and supernaturally the Spirit of God changed the natural laws of time and set us in the hospital parking lot in record time.

The power of the Holy Spirit has not diminished in these last days. The same Spirit that transported Elijah in the Old Testament (2 Kings 2:11) and Philip in the New Testament (Acts 8:39-40) can transport you in this day and age if it completes His divine purpose.

Miracles for the Benefit of All

The Bible says that everything was created through the Word (Jesus) and for the Word (Colossians 1:16). You were created for Him, and He wants the best for you. And through the church, He intends for the world to be blessed.

The working of miracles is one way God can bless the world. He can supernaturally bless you and He can supernaturally bless the church. To the church He has given gifts that are a blessing and one of the gifts is the working of miracles.

The gift of the working of miracles is available for the church today. As a Christian, you have been qualified by the blood of Jesus. As you open your heart to receive the working of His power and step out in faith, you become a candidate for this miraculous gift. The gift is prepared. The Spirit of God is moving over the face of the earth looking for those who are willing to receive.

CHAPTER 13

THE GIFT OF PROPHECY
Sixth Gift

But the manifestation of the Spirit is given to each
one for the profit of all ... to another prophecy ...

1 Corinthians 12:7,10

Definition: The gift of prophecy is the supernatural utterance of the things of God in a known language.

When God speaks to an individual or to a group by way of the gift of prophecy, He imparts knowledge, wisdom, understanding, and instruction to an individual, group, to the church, or to a nation. This prophetic word from the heart of God is supernaturally delivered through a person that the Holy Spirit has chosen to speak through. As the words from God flow through the speaker unedited and pure, they will be pure life and reveal the heart and will of God for the hearer.

This gift is the most prominent of the three gifts of speech because it takes the other two gifts (tongues and interpretation of tongues) to equal it (1 Corinthians 14:5).

Jesus said that the Holy Spirit would reveal things to come. Many times this revelation comes through the gift of prophecy.

> **Do not quench the Spirit; do not despise prophetic utterances. But examine everything carefully; hold fast to that which is good.**
>
> **1 Thessalonians 5:19-21 (NASB)**

The Parallel Flow

There is the natural flow of prophecy where an individual teaches from the written Word of God and speaks God's known written will. All believers can prophesy and should be saying what God says.

However, the supernatural gift of the Holy Spirit called the gift of prophecy is a supernatural utterance when the Holy Spirit guides the one prophesying with words that do not come from the speaker's mind. They are not learned or studied, but they are words by the Spirit of God that are given to edify the church.

Judging Prophecy

The gift of prophecy in operation by the Holy Spirit will not bring depression or despair, but will lift up, build up, and strengthen the body of Christ on earth.

> **Pursue love, and desire spiritual gifts, but especially that you may prophesy. For he who speaks in a tongue does not speak to men but to God, for no one**

understands him; however, in the spirit he speaks mysteries.

But he who prophesies speaks edification and exhortation and comfort to men. He who speaks in a tongue edifies himself, but he who prophesies edifies the church.

I wish you all spoke with tongues, but even more that you prophesied; for he who prophesies is greater than he who speaks with tongues, unless indeed he interprets, that the church may receive edification.

1 Corinthians 14:1-5

First Corinthians 14:29 says, *"Let two or three prophets speak, and let the others pass judgment."* This brings us to the question: "How do we judge prophecy?" If someone is standing and prophesying, how do we know if it is of God or not?

First, we must remember that the Spirit of God always ministers through peace and restoration and not through fear and condemnation.

All prophecy must lift up and exalt Jesus. Any prophecy that lifts up a person or an organization above Jesus is not of God. A false prophecy will always try to divert the glory, the honor, and the attention to another individual or group. (1 John 4:1-3.)

All spoken prophecy must agree with God's written Word. Any prophecy that does not agree is false.

We must hold every prophecy up to the test of First Corinthians 14:3 where it says that he who prophesies speaks edification and exhortation and comfort to men. Prophecies are given through the anointing of the Holy Spirit and will always produce liberty and be soaked in love. If a "prophet" speaks fear and condemnation, then reject that prophecy. It is not of God.

Qualified to Prophesy

The apostle Peter explained how prophecy is derived. He said, *"For prophecy never came by the will of man, but holy men of God spoke as they were moved by the Holy Spirit"* (2 Peter 1:21).

When teaching concerning the gift of prophecy, a question that is almost always asked is this: Who is qualified to prophesy? When it comes to prophecy as the gift of the Holy Spirit, this question is somewhat irrelevant. While holiness always creates an atmosphere for the Holy Spirit, ultimately He distributes the gift to whom He desires. He is the one who qualifies and decides to whom the gift will be given.

From my many years of experience and from biblical precedent, I can safely say that the Holy Spirit does not always pick the person I think He should pick. In other words, the understanding of man must submit to the will of God and allow the Spirit of God to do His will.

The Office of a Prophet

In the New Testament church, one of the offices is the office of a prophet. This office is not attained through education or by the intellect of man, but is bestowed upon the person God chooses who submits and receives this office. A person who sits in the office of a prophet is himself a gift to the church.

And He Himself gave some to be apostles, some prophets, some evangelists, and some pastors and teachers, for the equipping of the saints for the work of ministry, for the edifying of the body of Christ.

Ephesians 4:11-12

In Acts 21 there is the story of Paul's companions who went to the house of Philip the evangelist in Caesarea. Philip had four daughters who prophesied. Also at Philip's house there was a prophet named Agabus who came down from Judea. While the four daughters prophesied, the Scriptures do not call them prophets, but Agabus is named as a prophet (v.10).

This passage reveals the truth that even though someone speaks the Word of God (which is the natural flow of prophecy), it doesn't mean they are called of God as a prophet. The office of a prophet is a position and not the same thing as the gift of prophecy. Prophesying alone does not make someone a prophet. A prophet prophesies, but everyone who prophesies is not a prophet.

The Prophecy of Jesus Concerning the Church

And these signs will follow those who believe: In My name they will cast out demons; they will speak with new tongues; they will take up serpents; and if they drink anything deadly, it will by no means hurt them; they will lay hands on the sick, and they will recover.

Mark 16:17-18

For forty days after His resurrection He appeared to His disciples and He taught them. He gave them instruction on what they were to do after He would depart. He said that those who believed and had been baptized would be saved and those who disbelieved would be condemned. He concluded by stating that there would be signs or attesting miracles that would accompany those who believe.

On the day Jesus proclaimed this, the church was only forty days old and He was instructing these new believers that as they went and proclaimed the gospel, they had been given the authority to cast out demons. He went on to say that if they were bitten by serpents or if they were poisoned, they would not be hurt because they were being sent on a mission to lay hands on the sick so that they could recover.

We can see this prophecy fulfilled in so many ways. First, the disciples went into the world preaching the gospel and everyone who believed was saved and delivered from condemnation. The book of Acts tells us that they turned the world upside down (Acts 17:6). They cast out demons and starting on the Day of Pentecost, they spoke with new tongues.

The Prophecy Fulfilled

While on the Island of Malta on a mission for God, a serpent attached itself to Paul's hand. The local people watched believing that he would die. However, Paul shook the serpent off into the fire and continued in the ministry with no harm coming to him. (Acts 28:3-6.)

Recently I spoke at a Holy Spirit conference on the Island of Malta. I saw the place where Paul was imprisoned and the recently-discovered anchor that had been thrown overboard when Paul was shipwrecked. When I asked my friend, who had been born and raised on the Island of Malta, about the poisonous viper that attached itself to Paul's hand, he told me that, according to local legend, when Paul shook it off and threw it into the fire, all the poisonous snakes on the island died. It is a fact that today there are no venomous snakes on the island nation of Malta.

Several attempts were made to kill John, the author of the Revelation of Jesus Christ, but they were unsuccessful. Nothing could by any means hurt him.

Jesus prophesied that the church would cast out demons, speak with new tongues, and be protected. His prophecy has been fulfilled and continues to be fulfilled today in the lives of those who believe.

"And these signs will follow those who believe."
—Jesus

Desire the Gift of Prophecy

The gift of prophecy is a direct message from the heart of God to man. When the prophetic word is heard and applied, it will always bring edification, exhortation, comfort and the end result will always be deliverance, restoration, and healing. The message will always be bathed in love and exalt the name of Jesus. It will bring peace and assurance to the hearer. For this reason, we should take the advice of Paul and desire prophecy.

CHAPTER 14

THE GIFT OF THE DISCERNING OF SPIRITS
Seventh Gift

> But the manifestation of the Spirit is given to each
> one for the profit of all ... to another discerning of
> spirits ...
>
> ### 1 Corinthians 12:7,10

*D*efinition: Discerning of spirits is the ability to see into the spirit world and understand the source and purpose of a spirit.

Years ago Charles Capps told me that sometimes it helps to understand what something is by also looking at what it is not. With this in mind, discerning of spirits is not discerning of devils or discerning of evil spirits. This would imply there is only one thing you can see in this gift and that is evil. Supernatural manifestations can come from two sources—from a good God or from a bad devil. One version of the Bible calls this gift "the distinguishing of spirits" (1 Corinthians 12:10 NASB).

The gifts are not given to make you look good. In fact, if the gift in operation glorifies the person receiving it more than it glorifies God, it probably is not from God.

It is not a type of spiritual mind reading or psychological insight. It is not the power to discern the faults of others or to judge them.

The gift of discerning of spirits is not the gift of discernment. I have heard people say that they had the gift of discernment, and through it they judge other people. There is not a gift of discernment and there is not a gift of judging. The gift of discerning of spirits is the ability to see into the realm of the spirit world and know the spiritual source of a physical manifestation.

The Parallel Flow

Many times it is obvious that the spirit behind a project or an event is not of God. In these cases, we are to use the authority we have been given by the Word of God. However, the gift of discerning of spirits is given by the Holy Spirit. To use our authority is our choice. To operate in the gift is submission to the will of the Spirit.

> **Behold, I give you the authority to trample on serpents and scorpions, and over all the power of the enemy, and nothing shall by any means hurt you.**
>
> **Luke 10:19**

After an evening meeting in a southern Missouri town, I needed fuel and a snack before taking the long drive home.

While looking for a place to get a sandwich, I pulled off the road at a small shopping center. It was late at night and all the shops were closed, but one shop had left all of its neon signs turned on. In the window were occult signs and symbols, a neon outline of a large hand, and a lighted sign that said, "Palm Reading Here."

Although it was late at night and I needed fuel for my car and I was hungry, none of that mattered. Something had exploded inside of me and I was on a mission! I got out of my car, I walked to the storefront, and I stood in front of the large plate glass window in front of the sign that said "Palm Reading Here." With the palms of my two hands outstretched, I placed them on the large palm on the window and I cursed that demonic business in the name of Jesus. I got back into my car, found a gas station, got a snack, and then drove several hours home.

Two weeks later I had another meeting in the same town, and as I drove into the town, I looked toward the shopping center. I noticed that the storefront that had housed the palm reader was now empty. The signs were gone, the windows were clean and a new sign hung in the window that said, "For Lease." This was a miracle, but it was a natural result of a believer using his authority.

As Christians, we have authority over all the power of the enemy. We have been given that authority by the Lord Jesus. It does not require a gift of the Spirit to use this authority, but simply requires the leading of the Spirit to know when to take it. Some Christians have the attitude—"Somebody

should do something about that store that sells pornography."
If you are a born-again believer, you have been empowered
and you are that somebody. Darkness has no power, but only
operates when light is absent. You are the light of the world
and Jesus said to let your light shine.

Seeing into the Spirit Realm

In the early years of our church, we were without our own
church building and rented a theater and several stores in a
shopping center. The theater had a thousand seats and a large
stage and because the floor was slanted with fixed seating,
during times of ministry we used the platform that was ele-
vated approximately four feet above the theater floor.

While ministering in one of the services, people would
come to the center of the stage where I would lay hands on
them and minister to them, and then they would walk off the
other side of the stage.

After ministering to one individual, I looked to the right
and a prominent lady from our community was standing there
waiting for the usher to bring her to center stage. I noticed
to her right a creature, which looked like a large slimy gray-
ish-green dog, sitting on the floor with its three-foot long
front legs straight out in front of it. I could see it clearly. The
lighting on the stage was good and I have 20-20 vision without glasses. There was no mistake. A dark green slimy creature
was poised, sitting tall at this woman's right hand, and I knew
that it was a demonic spirit.

While it appeared I was pointing at the woman about fifteen feet away, I was actually pointing at the creature standing

next to her and I commanded it to go, in the name of Jesus. It leaped off of the platform to the auditorium floor four feet below. It ran in a galloping style up the aisle and through the doors at the back of the auditorium.

It was only when I looked back at the prominent woman and saw by the look on her face that she thought I was talking to her, that I realized I was the only one who had seen the spirit.

The meeting continued and there was good ministry, but the Holy Spirit revealed another truth to me that day. When the gift of discerning of spirits is imparted and you can see into the realm of the spirit, you may see things and understand things that no one else present can see or understand. When Paul was on the road to Damascus, he heard the discernable voice of the Lord, while those with him did not (Acts 22:9).

In my fifty years of ministry, this was the only time I have seen a demonic spirit clearly. While there have been countless times I have encountered demonic spirits and seen physical manifestations within other people, this was the only time I've seen one separately.

So why did the Holy Spirit reveal the physical presence of a demon to me that day? First, it made me realize that demonic spirits can actually be in a church service near where ministry is taking place. Secondly, it revealed the hideousness and grotesqueness of who they really are. And third, I had direct visual confirmation that when I told it to leave, it had no choice. It had to leave. These truths have helped me in ministry.

The Anointing Stirs Up Demonic Spirits

When word gets out that the gifts of the Holy Spirit are manifest in a ministry, it draws people who need deliverance from the bondage of the enemy, whether it be physical, financial, or emotional. But sometimes there are those sent by the enemy to disrupt and to distract from what the Holy Spirit desires to accomplish.

Paul had this happen in his ministry. In Acts chapter 16, Paul and Silas were on their way to prayer when they were met by a young female slave who had a spirit and she was able to predict future events. Because of this demonic trickery, she earned a great deal of money for her owners. She was known as a fortune teller.

The young girl followed Paul and Silas around proclaiming, "These men are servants of the Most High God who are telling men how to be saved" (v.17). She didn't just say this once, but many times, and she continued doing this for many days. Understandably, after a time Paul became greatly annoyed. Even though she may have been saying something that sounded right, her continued proclamation without end for a period of days was actually disruptive and a hindrance to what Paul was trying to do.

So when Paul had enough of the annoyance, he turned and spoke to the spirit that was possessing the young girl and he said, *"I command you in the name of Jesus Christ to come out of her"* (v.18). And within the hour the spirit was gone.

While being released from the possession of a demonic spirit may have been a breath of freshness for the slave girl, the ones who owned her didn't see it quite that way. Without the demonic spirit, her ability to be a fortune teller was gone, along with her master's ability to con people out of their money. Her masters seized Paul and Silas and had them imprisoned.

While the story of Paul and Silas continues and is very interesting, the point I wanted to make is this. Their anointing to bring deliverance and set the captives free not only drew the sick and diseased who wanted deliverance, but also drew demonic spirits whose purpose was to hinder their ministry. In the same way that the gifts of the Spirit did not pass away with the first century church, neither has the attempt of the enemy to disrupt a move of God.

Disruptions

One time, while I was speaking at a convention in Iowa, there was a young man in his thirties who was sitting near the back of the auditorium. This young man had the build of a football lineman. In the middle of my preaching, he stood up and started running to the platform. He ran up the steps onto the stage and threw his arms around me in a bear hug.

The audience was silent as they watched this young guy squeezing me so tightly that I couldn't move. Because I was holding the microphone in my right hand, the microphone was pressed between his chest and mine. There was no wiggle room. When he drew close to my ear and whispered, "I love you," I heard the Spirit of God say, "Speak My name." So in a normal voice, I said, "Jesus." When I spoke the name of Jesus, he screamed and leaned back, but still had a firm grip on my body.

Because he had leaned back, my hand was loosened just a little. I touched his head and spoke the name Jesus again. Once again, he shrieked and leaned back a little further.

This time I was free and a third time I said, "Jesus." Then something totally unexpected happened. Both of his hands went over his head until he was in a backbend in front of all the people. His feet were on the floor and his hands were on the floor and his back was arched.

He was wearing a t-shirt and it didn't stretch all the way to his pants. His chubby tummy and belly button were exposed and were the highest part of his body. Then I slapped my hand onto his stomach and I said, "I rebuke you foul spirit. Be delivered in the name of Jesus."

At that moment this big young man fell to the floor and started flopping like a fish. Looking back on what happened, it could almost seem comical—a room full of church people bussed in from several denominational churches with one of their own on the platform flopping around with arms and legs going everywhere.

When you are under the anointing of the Holy Spirit, there is no fear of demonic spirits. There were others on the platform that day and I calmly turned to a young bearded man and said, "Would you take this man out of here?" To my surprise, he stood up, threw up both hands and said, "I'm not touching that guy."

What I did not know was that the young bearded man on the platform was a guest of his brother, who was a strong Christian; however, the young man on the platform had rarely even been to church.

I remember looking at the back of the auditorium and seeing the hotel chef and his assistant wearing their tall chef hats, like a picture from a magazine, standing in the doorway. One of them was even holding a large wooden spoon. Evidently the commotion drew the attention of the kitchen staff at the hotel. All eyes were on me and the young man flopping on the floor.

Eventually two ministers came and they literally drug the man out of the auditorium. By this time he was exhausted and limp. Without missing a beat, I continued with my message and I truly believe many lives were changed that night.

What Was Meant For Evil, Became Good

As the service was drawing to a close, the two ministers that had taken the young man out brought him back into the auditorium. The young man walked to the front where he briefly gave his testimony about how he and some of his friends from church attended the meeting for the sole purpose of making fun of speaking in tongues. But during the service something came over him and he lost control of himself.

When the two ministers took him to the back room, he was delivered from bondage and he said he had never felt so free. What the devil meant for evil, the power of the Spirit of God turned around, and it actually became a great testimony.

A few weeks later while I was sitting in the library at my home, I received a phone call from the young bearded man on the platform who was the guest of his brother. He told me that as a result of what took place that night, his life had changed completely. He felt he should go into the ministry and wanted to know if I knew of a good Bible school he could attend. I directed him to a school that I trusted would teach him the true Word of God. He enrolled, attended, and graduated from this Bible college and has been in full time Christian ministry as a missionary in a foreign nation ever since.

From the Day of Pentecost the working of the Holy Spirit has not changed, but likewise neither has the work of the devil. As Christians, we must never forget that we have been given authority over all the power of the enemy and that as Jesus prophesied, nothing by any means shall harm us.

Discerning False Prophecies

I am currently the pastor of a growing church that overlooks the Lake of the Ozarks. With a full-size working lighthouse and sitting on 45 acres of land, our church is solidly established within the community. However, the church started out as a Bible study in a hotel.

As our church began to grow, outside forces came along and attempted to take control. Three men from a large ministry in Kansas City wanted to meet with me. They proceeded to tell me how our new church was to submit to their ministry and how they would oversee our church to help it grow. I had never met these three men and only had a distant knowledge of the ministry they represented. I felt no leading by the Holy Spirit whatsoever to be a part of their ministry and rejected their offer.

During this same time, a woman started attending our young church and asked for a meeting with me. I had no knowledge of this woman before she attended our church. At the meeting she told me that she knew she had been called as a prophetess. She said God had instructed her to write my sermons for me and give them to me each week so I could present them to the congregation.

It was at that moment that I realized that I was much smarter than the devil thought I was. Again, I rejected her offer and she quit attending our church.

The point of these two stories is very basic and simple. When you step out to do the work that God has told you to do, the enemy will use every method he can to stop what you are called to do. It is critical to be led by the Holy Spirit and not by human logic. While the plans and words of the enemy can sound intriguing, you will not attain the success in God's plan for your life and ministry unless you are led by the Holy Spirit.

Demonic Spirits

Now it happened on a certain day, as He was teaching, that there were Pharisees and teachers of the law sitting by, who had come out of every town of Galilee, Judea, and Jerusalem. And the power of the Lord was present to heal them.

Luke 5:17

In the same way that we can sense that the Spirit of the Lord is present to heal and perform life-changing miracles, so can demonic spirits. For centuries, demons who live in the spirit world have seen the miraculous power of God being manifest in the physical world. When they anticipate someone's deliverance is at hand, they do everything within their power to stop it.

Demonic spirits are fallen angels who have already been judged and sentenced to eternal torment in a place created for them called hell (Matthew 25:41). These spirits are tormented and have nothing to lose. They hate God's creation. Mankind has been provided with a way through the blood of Jesus to receive eternal life and experience the glory of God forever in God's eternal kingdom. There is no deliverance or salvation for these angels that rebelled against God in heaven, and while waiting for the execution of their sentence, in their frenzy, they seek to torment mankind (Matthew 8:29).

Over decades of ministry, I have learned that when a demonic manifestation takes place, we are not to be disturbed or distracted. It usually means that a miracle is at hand and the forces of darkness are attempting to derail or prevent the miracle.

Snake Lady

Such was the case at the meeting in Quincy, Illinois. That evening a great supernatural miracle took place in the life of a crippled man. (See chapter 10.) Moments before the miracle took place, a woman at the front of the church allowed a demonic spirit to control her. Her body began slithering like a snake. She even made hissing sounds as her tongue moved side to side.

I knew my authority and the temptation was to cast the demonic spirit out of her. But I heard the Spirit of God say,

"Have another minister deal with her. I want your focus on someone else." I turned to another minister and said, "Take care of this."

I walked across the stage to minister to the crippled man, and saw the greatest physical miracle I have ever seen. But twenty feet away I could hear the snake lady hissing as the other minister was commanding the spirit to leave her.

Why did this demonic manifestation occur? It was obviously to distract me from receiving the gift of miracles, the gift of healing, and the gift of faith that was in operation when a man who was crippled and deformed from birth was completely restored and healed to a perfectly normal body.

While Christians are commissioned to cast out demons, we must remember that all of the demons who were on earth at the time of Jesus are still here. Some of them have been cast out multiple times and even though they were cast out, they are still on the earth awaiting their execution date. So, we cannot allow demonic spirits to be a distraction when God has given us a mission to accomplish.

While the Holy Spirit was preparing to use the gift of faith, the gift of healing, and the gift of miracles, He imparted the gift of discerning of spirits while on the way to use the other three gifts.

The Holy Spirit Reveals the Hidden

Years ago, my parents and I had an opportunity to be involved in a business deal that was designed to put a million dollars into our family business and deliver us from impending disaster. It looked like a good deal. Everybody told us it was a good deal. We had driven a long way to this meeting to sign the papers.

As we were sitting at the table getting ready to sign, I heard the Spirit of God speak to my heart and say, "Don't do it." I had to discern the spirit. The gift of discerning of spirits came upon me and I knew that it was the Spirit of God saying, "Don't do it." My parents also sensed that we should not sign.

The businessman and his lawyer were stunned when I backed up from the table and said, "I'm sorry, we can't sign this." He said, "Why? This is a bonanza deal for you!" This businessman claimed to be a great Christian. But we didn't sign the papers.

Later we found out that he was a professional con artist and his scheme was to steal businesses owned by Christians by pretending to be a Christian. He knew all the Christian phrases to speak, and how to appear as a Christian, but in the fine print of his contracts, his victims would end up losing everything.

Discerning of spirits can deliver you from financial disaster!

You Can't Cast Out the Flesh

Demonic manifestations and evil activities of the flesh some-times appear the same, so it is very important that when we minister to a person that we know if the root of their prob-lem is demonic or flesh. You can command devils away from a person, but if the deeds of the flesh have developed into a learned behavior, then casting out spirits that aren't even there will not obtain any results.

While one person may throw a temper fit and cause disruption because they are under the control of a demonic spirit, another person can throw a temper fit that appears similar. But the second person may be doing it because it has become a part of their lifestyle and they have learned over the years that by throwing a fit, they can control other people.

When ministering by the Holy Spirit, it is imperative to know the difference. If you will not quench the Spirit, the Holy Spirit will usually impart the gift of discerning of spirits and your ability to minister will be increased.

Likewise, a sickness may be physical and the gift of healing is required for deliverance; but the same symptoms may appear in another person and it is not a physical sickness, but a demonic manifestation or the spirit of sickness. A physical sickness is not cast out, but is healed and a spiritual sickness is not healed, but cast out. Either way, the result is good and there is a need for the gift of discerning of spirits.

Exposing the Spirit World

While speaking at a convention in Ottumwa, Iowa, between meetings my wife and I were being escorted up a stairwell to the green room where we would be able to refresh ourselves between sessions. In the stairwell, we encountered another minister who was at the convention. As we had never met, I stretched out my hand to greet him and introduce myself. He immediately recoiled back against the wall and said, "It's an honor to meet you, Brother Ollison, but I cannot touch your hand. I have a gift from God that whenever I touch someone, I know everything about their life."

As I stood there in amazement listening to a strange story about how he had exposed the life of another person through this "gift," I realized this so-called minister was entertaining demonic spirits and claiming it was a gift from God.

I was operating in the gift of discerning of spirits. That gift had been imparted to me at that moment by the Holy Spirit. I knew the truth about this man's "gift." Although it was evident through my years of experience that this man was being led by demonic spirits, the gift of discerning of spirits confirmed it.

> For such are false apostles, deceitful workers, trans-forming themselves into apostles of Christ. And no wonder! For Satan himself transforms himself into an angel of light. Therefore it is no great thing if min-isters also transform themselves into ministers of righteousness, whose end will be according to their works.
>
> 2 Corinthians 11:13-15

All Christians have been given the commission to minister the gospel to the world. By having the availability of discern-ing of spirits, your ministry will be more powerful. While we are instructed in the Scriptures how to take authority over the power of the enemy, the gift of discerning of spirits will assist us by clearly exposing the spirit world.

But we belong to God, and those who know God listen to us. If they do not belong to God, they do not listen to us. That is how we know if someone has the Spirit of truth or the spirit of deception.

1 John 4:6 NLT

CHAPTER 15

THE GIFT OF DIFFERENT KINDS OF TONGUES
Eighth Gift

But the manifestation of the Spirit is given to each one for the profit of all ... to another different kinds of tongues ...

1 Corinthians 12:7,10

Definition: Different kinds of tongues is the supernatural utterance by the Holy Spirit in languages never learned by the speaker or understood by the mind of the speaker, and not necessarily understood by the hearer.

The most controversial and misunderstood gift of the nine gifts has been the gift of different kinds of tongues. Much of the misunderstanding and confusion comes from not understanding the difference between praying in tongues (praying in the spirit) and the gift of different kinds of tongues. While these two types of New Testament tongues appear to be the same by the casual observer, scripturally they have different objectives and different administration.

Although praying in tongues and the gift of different kinds of tongues have differences that will be explained later in this chapter, both are only available after a Christian has received the baptism of the Holy Spirit.

The Parallel Flow

Operating in the gift of "different kinds of tongues" may sound or even seem the same as praying in tongues (praying in the spirit), but is actually quite different. While you can pray in the spirit (in tongues) anytime you want and there does not need to be an interpretation, the gift of different kinds of tongues is given by the Holy Spirit as He desires. The gift of tongues requires interpretation of tongues (another gift) in order to benefit all.

Some denominations and ministries teach against the gifts of the Spirit and seem to focus on what they call the "error of tongues." Sadly, because they don't understand the parallel flow of the Spirit, they lump praying in the spirit and the gift of speaking in tongues together as the same thing. Until this basic difference is understood, the scriptures on the gifts will seem confusing. While it is true that some groups are in error concerning tongues, this alone should not be used as an excuse to avoid tongues.

In the early days of my ministry, I was approached by a minister who bragged and proudly proclaimed that in his church he had never allowed anyone to teach about the gift of tongues. When I asked him why, his response was, "Ninety percent of those people are faking it and doing it wrong." I was young and did not want to rebuke an elder, but I thought to myself, "So what if ninety percent are in error? What about the ten percent that are not?" By his own admission, he was stating that there was a ten percent remnant that was moving properly in the gift of tongues. We should never cease proclaiming a truth because someone else is proclaiming it incorrectly.

Remember, praying in the spirit is something you decide to do. Operating in the gift of tongues is something the Holy Spirit decides you are going to do and you yield to His will and His gift.

How They Are Different

Before we examine these two spiritual actions in greater detail, let me give you a brief overview of how they are different.

In this book, when we use the phrase *the gift of tongues*, we are directly referring to the gift of different kinds of tongues. The gift of tongues is given by the Holy Spirit to a Christian who has made themselves available through spiritual and physical submission. With this gift, the Holy Spirit speaks through the individual who is the recipient of the gift. The recipient cannot activate this gift at will because the Holy Spirit distributes this gift when and to whom He desires.

But one and the same Spirit works all these things, distributing to each one individually as He wills.

1 Corinthians 12:11

As the Holy Spirit speaks through the recipient, they should pray to receive the gift of interpretation of tongues;

however, it is the Holy Spirit who ultimately decides who will receive the gift of interpretation. The gift of tongues should always be followed with the gift of interpretation and the interpretation is directed to an individual or group.

Praying in tongues, or praying in the spirit, is initiated by the one praying and by their own will. One who prays in the spirit is not speaking a message to an individual or group, but rather is speaking to God (1 Corinthians 14:2). While praying in the spirit to God, the individual praying does not have an understanding of what he is praying for. However, the Spirit assists in the prayer, and prays the will of God and when the will of God is prayed, the prayer is answered even though the individual praying does not know what he is praying for (1 John 5:14-15).

The Gift of Tongues

Of all the nine spiritual gifts, the gift of tongues is the most publicized, exalted, and ridiculed. Like on the Day of Pentecost when the 120 left the upper room and began speaking in the gift of tongues under the anointing of the Holy Spirit, the manifestation was so bizarre that there was no middle ground. People either received the word that was spoken and were baptized, or they ridiculed, pointing their fingers at the believers and saying, "These people are drunk!" (Acts 2:13).

Likewise, today when the gift of tongues is in operation, a choice must be made. Do we receive the supernatural manifestation of God speaking to us, or do we reject it as foolishness? Sadly, many Christians, through a lack of knowledge and understanding, have rejected this gift. In these latter days, as the church becomes brighter and the world becomes darker, God speaks through the church to His people and to the world through the gift of tongues and interpretation.

Diversities of Operation

Many years ago, I was told of a missionary who arrived in China with the purpose of being at an extremely important meeting. This meeting was time sensitive and it was critical that the missionary not be late. Upon arriving at the airport, the person who was to meet him and take him to the meeting was not there. The missionary could not speak one word of Chinese. His guide was to be his interpreter, but his guide was not there. Without an interpreter and not knowing the language, the missionary immediately decided to pray for guidance.

He didn't know how he should pray so he began praying in the spirit. Within moments, a taxi pulled up to the curb and the driver motioned for the man to get in. Assuming that his guide had sent the taxi, he got in the back seat of the cab and continued to pray in tongues. The taxi swerved in and out of traffic and finally made it across town and pulled up at the curb of exactly where he was supposed to be. An associate, who was also to be at the meeting, was standing on the curb as his taxi pulled up. He was shocked to see the missionary was there because his guide had failed to show up at the airport.

The missionary said that everything worked out okay and thanked his friend for sending the cab. His friend replied,

"We didn't send the cab." As the friend, who was fluent in Chinese, paid the taxi driver, he asked the driver in Chinese how he knew to bring the missionary to this place. The taxi driver replied in his native language, "The American sitting in the back seat guided me here. He told me every turn to take and he told me when to stop."

While this story may seem impossible to some, it is simply the same thing that happened on the Day of Pentecost. The Galileans in the upper room spilled into the streets speaking in tongues and everyone there heard them speaking the wonders of God in their own language. Likewise, the tongues spoken by the missionary in China were interpreted by the Holy Spirit in the ear of the taxi driver.

Varieties of Effects

While the missionary may have started praying in the spirit, the Holy Spirit took over and distributed the gift of tongues to the missionary. Without knowing it, he was giving the taxi driver directions on how to take him to this very important meeting. The missionary thought he was praying in the spirit, but it was actually the gift of tongues speaking through him to the cab driver. While this may be unusual, by praying in the spirit, the missionary was setting the atmosphere for the Holy Spirit to administer the gift of tongues.

We must remember that the full title of this gift of the Holy Spirit is *different kinds of tongues*, and just before Paul listed the nine gifts, he said there are varieties of gifts, varieties of ministries, and there are varieties of effects. This gift of various kinds or different kinds of tongues by its title alone lets us know that it may manifest itself in many different ways. Of course, the Holy Spirit knows more than we know and in any given situation He knows the best way to present His gift. As we yield to Him, that gift will be for the common good of everyone involved.

As a pastor, many times He has guided me during a church service to pray for someone and because I didn't know what to pray for, I would lay hands on them and pray in the spirit (Romans 8:26-27). While praying in the spirit, He would impart the gift and the result would be the gift of tongues and the gift of interpretation in operation, which resulted in a word of knowledge or a word of wisdom for the person being prayed for. Many times praying in the spirit sets the tone and creates the atmosphere for the distribution of the gifts.

> Now there are varieties of gifts, but the same Spirit. And there are varieties of ministries, and the same Lord. There are varieties of effects, but the same God who works all things in all persons. But to each one is given the manifestation of the Spirit for the common good.
>
> 1 Corinthians 12:4-7 (NASB)

The Gift Requires Interpretation

The gift of tongues can be in an unknown language or in a heavenly language, but either way, God is speaking to an individual or a group. The gift of tongues always requires another gift to be present—the gift of interpretation of tongues. While the Spirit is speaking through the recipient of the gift in an unknown language, that same person or another person will receive the interpretation and proclaim it boldly. The word spoken will be from God to man and it will bring comfort, exhortation, correction, or guidance. It will never be hateful or condemning because the source of the message is God and God is love.

Since the gift of tongues is God to speaking to man, without an interpretation, there would be no purpose. Paul said that when a person speaks in tongues, they should pray that they would receive the interpretation (1 Corinthians 14:13).

A Brief Review

As we have stated earlier, there are two basic types of tongues that have been given to the church. While they may appear to be the same to the uninformed observer, they are completely different in administration and purpose.

The gift of tongues is God speaking to man with various operations and effects through the will and specific direction of the Holy Spirit Himself. The gift of interpretation of tongues is designed to work with the gift of tongues.

Praying in tongues, which is also called praying in the spirit, is man speaking to God by his own will and is completely at the will of the one praying.

Praying in the Spirit

Being filled with the Holy Spirit opens the ability to pray supernaturally. There are times when we don't know how to pray because a situation or a decision is so great or devastating that it's not directly addressed in the Word of God. For example, your employment transfers you to a new city and you have found three houses that all look like they would meet your need. Because there is no way to tell in the natural which one to buy, you should pray in the spirit and the Spirit Himself, on your behalf, will intercede and pray the will of God for you.

> Likewise the Spirit also helps in our weaknesses. For we do not know what we should pray for as we ought, but the Spirit Himself makes intercession for us with groanings which cannot be uttered. Now He who searches the hearts knows what the mind of the Spirit is, because He makes intercession for the saints according to the will of God.
>
> Romans 8:26-27

Even though you may not know in your natural mind which house you're praying to receive, the Holy Spirit knows which one. It's God's will that you purchase the correct house that will meet the needs of your family and cause you the least problems with repairs, location, taxes, etc. While you do not know which house to pray for, the Holy Spirit does and by you praying in the spirit, with the Holy Spirit assisting you, you are now praying the will of God for you.

Again, when you are praying in the spirit, this is not one of the gifts of the Spirit and does not require interpretation. While it's always possible for the Holy Spirit to reveal the intent of the prayer, it's not required like it is with the gift. It takes faith to pray in the spirit because you are placing your trust in God without the evidence of understandable words. In fact, praying in the spirit cannot be interpreted because the intercession is too deep for words.

> **...but the Spirit Himself intercedes for us with groanings too deep for words.**
>
> **Romans 8:26 (NASB)**

Knowing the Will of God

When we pray, we must pray the will of God. Only when we pray His will, will He hear us. In fact, we are clearly told in First John 5:14 that we can ask anything according to His will, and He will hear us. Then in verse 15 we are told that if He hears us, He grants us the request. But we can never forget that He only hears our request if we ask according to His will. What is the will of God? His will is found in His Word, the Holy Bible, and by praying in the spirit.

Through the years as pastor, I have had countless meetings with people who were going through trials in their lives. Some of these trials were financial, some were emotional, and some were physical. When I would ask them if they had prayed concerning their situations, many times I would get the reply, "Yes, but I'm just not sure what God is going to do." Then I would usually ask them, "Why is it that you don't know what God would do?" And most of the time it was because they had not searched the Scriptures to find God's will or they kind of knew in a way what they thought God's will was. But because of bad teaching or being subject to church doctrines that were wrong, they did not have a firm understanding of God's plan for their life.

God is a good God and every good and perfect gift comes from Him (James 1:17). God wants to bless His children and even sent His Son, Jesus, to redeem them from the curse of the law (Galatians 3:13). Jesus came to preach good news to the poor and that good news is freedom from poverty. He preached healing to the sick and restoration to the broken hearted. So when it comes to certain things, we know the will of God and when we pray, there is not a need to only pray in tongues. Why? Because we know His will.

For example, if you are sick, we know that God said in Psalm 103:3 that *"I am the God who heals thee."* So when we pray, we pray to be healed.

If the problem is poverty, we know that God takes pleasure in the prosperity of His saints, so we pray for prosperity (Psalm 35:27).

If the problem is a broken heart or an emotional issue, we know that the Scripture says God sent Jesus to the earth and was anointed to heal the brokenhearted (Luke 4:18).

In all of these things, we can pray in the understanding with confidence because He has promised them to us, so obviously they must be His will for us. He wouldn't promise us something unless He desired for us to have it.

Now this is the confidence that we have in Him, that if we ask anything according to His will, He hears us. And if we know that He hears us, whatever we ask, we know that we have the petitions that we have asked of Him."

1 John 5:14-15

Ignoring One of the Greatest Spiritual Tools

Pray in the Spirit on all occasions with all kinds of prayers and requests. With this in mind, be alert and always keep on praying for all the Lord's people.

Ephesians 6:18 (NIV)

Much of the confusion about praying in the spirit and the gift of different kinds of tongues is because of avoidance, fear, and ignorance on the subject. It is impossible to attain wisdom and knowledge about tongues by ignoring what the Bible has to say about it. Because of past abuses and because of incorrect teaching, some ministries, pastors, and teachers have chosen to avoid anything in the Word concerning speaking in tongues.

This avoidance has left the church void of one of the greatest spiritual tools provided to the church today. Praying the will of God can literally protect your family, deliver you from destruction, and save your life.

Paul said in Second Corinthians 11:3 that the gospel was not complicated, but was actually quite simple. Anything avoided or feared will seem complicated, but understanding and truth bring clarity. For this reason, we must search the

Word, study, and understand what the Holy Spirit teaches us about tongues.

The great thing about praying the will of God is this. When we pray His will, we are assured that He hears us, and also that when He hears us, we know we receive our request. So when you pray in the spirit, you can be assured that you are praying His will and that He is committed to fulfilling that prayer.

Why Should I Pray in the Spirit?

But you, beloved, building yourselves up on your most holy faith, praying in the Holy Spirit.

Jude 1:20

The purpose of praying in the spirit is to pray the will of God and to strengthen yourself in the knowledge that you have prayed His will. One of the greatest ways to relieve stress and be filled with joy is through the building up that comes through praying in the spirit.

Some people refer to praying in the spirit as their prayer language. Paul said if we don't know how to pray, the Holy Spirit will intercede for us and pray the will of God on our behalf (Romans 8:26). The solution to your problem may be a mystery to you, but there are no mysteries in God. Even though you may not know what you are praying in your own consciousness, the Spirit does and He prays the will of God. God hears this prayer and acts to fulfill it.

Someone may ask, "Then why shouldn't I just pray in the spirit all the time? If I'm praying God's will when I'm praying in the spirit, then I will always be praying correctly." The answer to this is quite simple. Praying in the spirit cannot be used as a crutch or an excuse for not knowing the Word of God.

What is the conclusion? As a Christian, I pray in the spirit and I pray with the understanding. Only when we do both will our prayer life be complete.

> **For if I pray in a tongue, my spirit prays, but my understanding is unfruitful. What is the conclusion then? I will pray with the spirit, and I will also pray with the understanding.**
>
> 1 Corinthians 14:14-15

Praying in the spirit allows the Holy Spirit to intercede for you and praying in the understanding is praying out of the abundance of your own heart.

Receive the Answer to Your Mystery

"But we speak the wisdom of God in a mystery, the hidden wisdom which God ordained before the ages for our glory" (1 Corinthians 2:7). How do we speak the wisdom of God? How do we speak answers to the mysteries? *"For he who speaks in a tongue does not speak to men but to God, for no one understands him; however, in the spirit he speaks mysteries"* (1 Corinthians 14:2).

When we speak in an unknown tongue, we are speaking mysteries, wisdom, and answers. We are speaking the hidden wisdom that God has hidden for us in these last days. The mysteries flow out of us when we get in the presence of God, in the secret place, and worship Him. When we pray in an unknown tongue, the Spirit of God is interceding through us. He is using our voice. He is using our vocal chords, but He is speaking the perfect will of God.

> **These things we also speak, not in words which man's wisdom teaches but which the Holy Spirit teaches, comparing spiritual things with spiritual.**
>
> 1 Corinthians 2:13

As a born-again believer, we have the One living on the inside of us who knows everything that is happening on the outside of us. So doesn't it make sense for us to get into fellowship with Him, to get into His presence, and pray in the spirit so we can pray the answer to hidden mysteries?

If something is happening in your life and you don't have the answer, go into your secret place. Enter into praise and worship and the presence of God. Speak in your unknown tongue and receive the answer to the mystery in your heart. Take the time to release your faith while you are praying in the spirit. As you receive the mysteries of God, you will also receive peace and comfort knowing that God has deposited the answer in you.

Keep Your Battery Charged

A battery contains power, but if a battery is left uncharged or unused, the power will diminish, which can be disastrous in times of emergency. During a storm is not the time to discover the batteries in your flashlight are dead.

Likewise, we must keep our spiritual battery full of faith by filling it with the Word so that in times of peril, we will not be caught off guard. The Holy Spirit is the power of God and by praying in the Spirit, we build up our most holy faith (Jude 1:20). Faith is the catalyst that activates God's miraculous supernatural power.

Being filled with the Holy Spirit is not a one-time event and then it's over. The apostles were filled with the Holy Spirit in the upper room with the evidence of speaking in tongues. Their boldness brought the wrath of the chief priests and the elders and they were commanded to not speak or teach at all in the name of Jesus (Acts 4:18). Upon telling their friends what had happened, they prayed and were all filled with the Holy Spirit again.

And when they had prayed, the place where they were assembled together was shaken; and they were all filled with the Holy Spirit, and they spoke the word of God with boldness.

Acts 4:31

In Ephesians 5:18 Paul admonishes the church to be filled with the Holy Spirit. The Greek word used there is *plerousthe*. The literal translation of this verb can best be stated as "be being kept filled." Billy Graham, the great American evangelist, in his book, *The Holy Spirit*, said that Ephesians 5:18 literally says, "Keep on being filled with the Spirit."[4] In his book, he also said, "Unfortunately millions of God's people do not enjoy the unlimited spiritual wealth at their disposal because they are not filled with the Holy Spirit. We are not

4 Billy Graham, *The Holy Spirit*, (Nashville: Thomas Nelson, 1988), 117.

filled once for all, like a bucket. Instead, we are to be filled constantly."[5] This would indicate that as believers we are to keep ourselves constantly filled as we live our lives each day. This process is how we daily are led by and walk by the Spirit.

And do not be drunk with wine, in which is dissipation; but be filled with the Spirit.

Ephesians 5:18

So keep your spiritual battery charged with the Word and by praying in the spirit.

Tongues + Interpretation = Prophecy

The apostle Paul said we should pursue love and desire spiritual gifts, but more than anything we should desire to prophesy because one who prophesies speaks edification, exhortation, and comfort to men and edifies the church. On the other hand, one who speaks in a tongue and speaks to God instead of men is praying in the spirit. Because he is praying in the spirit and there is no interpretation, his words are mysteries and he is edifying himself.

He who speaks in a tongue edifies himself, but he who prophesies edifies the church.

1 Corinthians 14:4

While praying in the spirit is necessary in the life of a Christian, in a public setting it can cause confusion. Paul is simply saying that for one person to speak the oracles of God

---

5 Ibid., 117.

in a church service is better than many people praying in the spirit loudly and disorderly. Confusion is eliminated and the whole church is edified. Praying in the spirit corporately is acceptable, but must be done at the instruction of the church leader or pastor.

He continues by saying that he desires that everyone would speak with tongues. But even more that they prophesied, for one who prophesies is greater than one who speaks with tongues. But we can't stop the sentence there. He adds a condition. He said one who prophesies is greater than one who speaks with tongues—unless he interprets. When tongues and interpretation are in operation as gifts of the Holy Spirit, they are equal to prophecy and he goes on to say the church receives edification. Praying in the spirit is personal, but the gift of tongues and the gift of interpretation are public and equal to prophecy (1 Corinthians 14:5).

Paul summed it up this way. He said, "If I come to you speaking in tongues, how will it profit you unless I speak to you by revelation, by knowledge, by prophesying, or by teaching?" (1 Corinthians 14:6). For example, in battle, the trumpet makes a certain sound so that the soldiers know how to prepare for battle. But if the person with the trumpet plays random notes without order, the soldiers don't know what to do. Likewise, if someone speaks to you in an unknown language, you won't understand. So if someone speaks in a tongue by the guidance of the Holy Spirit, then he should pray that he will interpret and then the whole body will be edified.

That means that tongues are a sign of God's power, not for those who are unbelievers, but to those who already believe.

Preaching the word of God, on the other hand, is a sign of God's power to those who do not believe rather than to believers. So that, if at a full church meeting you are all speaking with tongues and men come in who are both uninstructed and without faith, will they not say that you are insane?

But if you are preaching God's word and such a man should come in to your meeting, he is convicted and challenged by your united speaking of the truth. His secrets are exposed and he will fall on his knees acknowledging God and saying that God is truly among you!

1 Corinthians 14:22-25 (PHILLIPS)

Remember, the gift of tongues with the gift of interpretation of tongues is a method God uses to speak to His children through the Holy Spirit. This gift is precious because through it we hear the heart of God.

CHAPTER 16

THE GIFT OF
INTERPRETATION OF TONGUES
Ninth Gift

But the manifestation of the Spirit is given to each one for the profit of all ... to another the interpretation of tongues. But one and the same Spirit works all these things, distributing to each one individually as He wills.

1 Corinthians 12:7,10,11

D*efinition:* The gift of the interpretation of tongues is the supernatural explanation by the Holy Spirit of the meaning of an utterance in an unknown tongue that is in an understandable language to the hearer.

I wish you all spoke with tongues, but even more that you prophesied; for he who prophesies is greater than he who speaks with tongues, unless indeed he interprets, that the church may receive edification.

> Therefore let him who speaks in a tongue pray that he may interpret.
>
> 1 Corinthians 14:5,13

The gift of interpretation of tongues is not the translation of tongues. When a language is written and converted to another language, it is translated. That is where you take individual words and convert them to their counterparts in the other language. This is not the case when interpreting tongues. The person receiving the gift, who may or may not be the person who presented the message in tongues, will speak by the guidance of the Holy Spirit and convey the meaning of the word spoken by the Holy Spirit.

The Parallel Flow

The parallel flow of the gift of interpretation of tongues is simply the revelation of the written Word of God by the Holy Spirit. While the gift of tongues requires the gift of interpretation to be of benefit to everyone, the revelation of the written Word of God comes through study and meditation. When we hide His Word in our hearts, the natural response for the Spirit of God is to bring revelation and understanding. This revelation is available to any believer who desires a greater depth in the Word of God.

While the Holy Spirit determines who will receive the gift of interpretation of tongues, the revelation of the Word is determined by the effort of each individual believer to apply themselves in the study of the Word. The Holy Spirit is always faithful to bring revelation.

The gift of interpretation of tongues is unique in that it can only be administered when the gift of tongues is in operation. The person receiving this gift must take a step of faith and begin speaking even though the entire interpretation has not yet been given by the Spirit at that time. As the one receiving the gift yields and speaks the words imparted to their spirit, the Holy Spirit continues to speak.

Remember, since the gift of tongues is God to speaking to man, without an interpretation, there would be no purpose. Let me explain.

A Step of Faith

Many years ago, I was the worship leader at a church that allowed the Holy Spirit to administer His gifts. In fact, I have always loved music. When I was fourteen years old my band recorded its first 45 rpm record at a studio in Kansas City. Through the years that followed, music was a very important part of my life.

Although I was the worship leader, I had only recently experienced the moving of the Holy Spirit. During one of our Sunday services and while the worship team was playing quietly between songs, the pastor acknowledged someone in the congregation and they started speaking with the gift of tongues. While they were speaking, the Holy Spirit revealed to me two very detailed sentences and I knew that this was the beginning of the interpretation. However, I also knew that there was more to it and I didn't know any more than beyond the two detailed sentences.

When the gift of tongues was complete, all was quiet. I wanted to speak because I knew the gift of interpretation had been imparted to me, but I didn't because I wanted to have it all before I opened my mouth. There was more silence and after what seemed like an eternity, the associate pastor of the church stood and said, "The Spirit of the Lord would say ..." and he proceeded to speak the two detailed sentences that I had in my heart that I knew were from God. But he didn't stop there. He continued with several more sentences and completed the interpretation. The gift of tongues and the interpretation of tongues had been given and received and the congregation was edified.

Later in a time of prayer, I asked the Lord why He only gave me a couple of sentences at the beginning of the interpretation while He gave the associate pastor the entire interpretation. The Lord spoke to my heart and this is what He said. "I didn't give the associate pastor any more than I gave you. He, unlike you, stepped out in faith and spoke what he had and as he spoke, I gave him more. You, on the other hand, quenched My Spirit."

While it was a great comfort to know that what I was hearing was from God because it was confirmed by the person who actually gave the interpretation, I was disappointed in myself that I had not stepped out in faith. That day was a great learning time for me. I realized how important it is for everything that is done by the Spirit to be done in faith. We must walk in the light we have been given and as we walk, the path will continue to be lighted ahead of us.

Since that day, I have had the gift of interpretation of tongues imparted to me many times, and in each instance the Holy Spirit only spoke to me a few words ahead of the words coming from my mouth. I believe that is wisdom on the part of the Holy Spirit because it is the nature of man to attempt to add his own explanations to what God says. This way the interpretation by the Holy Spirit is pure and undefiled by the thoughts of man.

The Spirit of Order

While it is the Spirit who gives utterance because the Holy Spirit is the one distributing the gift as He wills, the one who receives the gift is not a mindless robot without control. Through wisdom and prudence (common sense and good judgment) and by the prompting of the Holy Spirit, the one receiving the gift operates in the gift.

The Holy Spirit will never bring confusion or chaos. When the Holy Spirit has a word from God to be spoken in an unknown tongue and interpreted, it is for the purpose of deliverance, edification, or correction and must be able to be heard. Anyone who creates noise or confusion, so that the individual delivering the word from God is not able to be heard, is out of order.

For God is not the author of confusion but of peace, as in all the churches of the saints.

1 Corinthians 14:33

CHAPTER 17

THE FRUIT OF THE SPIRIT

But the fruit of the Spirit is love, joy, peace, longsuffering, kindness, goodness, faithfulness, gentleness,
self-control. Against such there is no law.

Galatians 5:22-23

T he fruit of the Spirit reveals the character of God and
because the Holy Spirit dwells within us, we now should
walk in the same characteristics. We know that God has not
given us the spirit of fear, but has given us the spirit of love,
power, and a sound mind (2 Timothy 1:7). Each portion of
the fruit of the Spirit reveals the heart of God and shows His
desire toward mankind. The fruit of the Spirit can be summed
up into one action that is the manifestation of love. After all,
God is love (1 John 4:16) and the Holy Spirit is His Spirit.

The Greatest is Love

He who does not love does not know God, for God
is love.

1 John 4:8

While there many places in the New Testament that talk about the gift of tongues, there are two chapters that are prominent in this teaching. They are First Corinthians 12, and First Corinthians 14. Sandwiched between these two chapters is First Corinthians 13, a chapter that is known for its teaching on love.

Chapter 13 starts out by saying, *"Though I speak with the tongues of men and of angels, but have not love, I have become as sounding brass or a clanging cymbal"* (v. 1). This opening verse clearly tells us that whether we speak in an earthly language or the heavenly language, our words must be soaked in agape love. If our words, whether earthly or heavenly, whether understandable or unintelligible, do not contain love, they are nothing but noise.

Then Paul goes on to say that even if he has the gift of prophecy and has the ability to understand all the mysteries and even if he can attain great knowledge, and even though he has mountain-moving faith, without love, he is nothing (v. 2).

But then he continues by talking about good works and how regardless of how good his works are, even if he sells everything and gives up everything so that others can be helped, if he doesn't have love, all of his actions are totally unprofitable (v. 3).

Then he gives the definition of love in great detail. When we examine this definition, we will find that it is very similar to the fruit of the Spirit listed in Galatians 5:22-23. Paul describes love this way. He says that love suffers long and is kind, that it does not envy and it's not arrogant, boastful, or puffed up. He said love does not behave rudely and does not think of itself first. It's not easily provoked and does not think about evil. This godly love does not rejoice when it sees sin, but rejoices in the truth. Love bears all things, believes all things, hopes all things, and endures all things. And then Paul sums up his definition by saying this, love never fails. (vv. 4-8.)

He continues by reminding us that prophecies, tongues, and knowledge are only for a temporary purpose and are a partial revelation of the full revelation we will someday receive. While faith, hope, and love are the pillars of our Christian walk, the greatest of the three is love. (vv. 9-13.)

As a young Christian, I would sometimes wonder why Paul interrupted his teaching on spiritual gifts with a teaching on love. But as the years have passed, I've come to understand that many divisions in the earthly organized church are a result of theological positions and doctrines with the absence of love. God is love and regardless of how great a ministry attempts to be or how spiritual they may appear, if love is absent, so is God.

When the nine parts of the fruit of the Spirit are united as one fruit, we could say this. The fruit of the Spirit is love.

The Three Groups

While the gifts of the Holy Spirit produce power, the fruit of the Spirit produces holiness. In the same way there are nine gifts of the Holy Spirit, there are also nine parts of the fruit of the Spirit. There are nine manifestations of the Holy Spirit through the gifts, and the fruit of the Spirit is revealed also in nine ways.

The gifts of the Holy Spirit can be grouped into three basic groups, and in the same way, the nine parts of the fruit of the Spirit can be grouped into three general groups.

These three groups are:

A. The foundation of who you are: love, joy, peace
B. Fruit of character: longsuffering, kindness, and goodness
C. Fruit that is displayed: faithfulness, gentleness, and self-control

The Foundation of Who You Are

The foundation of your character is what supports all that you do in life. A person who is grounded in love, joy, and peace will never be shaken by what they see because, regardless of the turmoil and chaos around them, they view life through the eyes of love, joy, and peace. Because God is love and because love was the motivation of God in sending His Son to redeem mankind, love is the key ingredient in the Christian lifestyle and true love never fails.

Love—Jesus said the greatest love man can have is to lay down his life for a friend. Likewise, the love of God is to lay down His life for mankind (1 John 3:16). The ultimate love of the universe is when the Creator of the universe lowers Himself to His creation and gives up His life in order to reconcile His creation back to Himself. Likewise as Christians, we are to walk in love toward each other as an example of the love of God.

Greater love has no one than this, than to lay down one's life for his friends.

John 15:13

A new commandment I give to you, that you love one another; as I have loved you, that you also love one another.

John 13:34

Joy—While happiness can be attained partially through the outward things of life, joy is internal. Happiness without joy is superficial, but the joy of the Lord that has been imparted to every born-again believer is the core of true happiness and strength.

Do not sorrow, for the joy of the Lord is your strength.

Nehemiah 8:10

These things I have spoken to you, that My joy may remain in you, and that your joy may be full.

John 15:11

Peace—There is earthly peace that comes from the absence of war and by the fulfillment of the natural desires of life. Having money in the bank, good health, and friends can bring a type of peace. Having true peace as a Christian comes from within and has nothing to do with the circumstances of life. Paul said that he had learned that he could be content (at peace) whether he had plenty or lack (Philippians 4:11). The peace that comes from our Lord and Savior, Jesus Christ is not the same as the peace that comes from the world.

> **Peace I leave with you, My peace I give to you; not as the world gives do I give to you. Let not your heart be troubled, neither let it be afraid.**
>
> **John 14:27**

> **For the kingdom of God is not eating and drinking, but righteousness and peace and joy in the Holy Spirit.**
>
> **Romans 14:17**

Fruit of Character

While love, joy, and peace are anchored deep within your spirit, patience, kindness, and goodness are the manifestations of the fruit of the Spirit that reach outside of yourself to the world. In relationships with others, these three are not for your benefit, but are for the people around you. They are key in ministry as you display patience, kindness, and goodness outward to others. When they are allowed to flow in full manifestation from the heart of a believer, they can heal and restore other people.

Longsuffering (Patience)—Let me give you the definition of a patient man. A patient man walks and talks the same way all the time. He walks like God and he talks like God. God is the God of peace, contentment, and patience and God is consistent in His character.

Patience is an attribute that must be active in the Christian lifestyle. Developing patience requires consistency. Consistency requires discipline and discipline requires obedience.

As a believer, we know that Jesus destroyed the works of the devil and through our faith, we have victory over the world. Because our born-again spirit knows that the victory has been obtained, there is no pressure of time and patience is the result.

For whatever is born of God overcomes the world. And this is the victory that has overcome the world— our faith.

1 John 5:4

That you may walk worthy of the Lord, fully pleasing Him, being fruitful in every good work and increasing in the knowledge of God; strengthened with all might, according to His glorious power, for all patience and longsuffering with joy.

Colossians 1:10-11

Kindness—As Christians we are commanded to be kind. Because we are created in the likeness and image of God, we as believers have been endowed with His character. He is our Father, He has been kind to us, and we should be like Him.

Love suffers long and is kind.

1 Corinthians 13:4

> Be kind to one another, tenderhearted, forgiving one
> another, even as God in Christ forgave you.
>
> Ephesians 4:32

Goodness—Goodness is manifest in benevolence to others—not just in word, but in deed. A good person helps the orphans and widows when they have needs. A good person makes sacrifices for a friend. When Moses asked God to reveal His glory, God showed him His goodness. The world will see the Father through your goodness and He will be glorified.

> Moses said, "Please, show me Your glory." Then He
> said, "I will make all My goodness pass before you,
> and I will proclaim the name of the Lord before you."
>
> Exodus 33:18-19

> Every good gift and every perfect gift is from above,
> and comes down from the Father of lights, with
> whom there is no variation or shadow of turning.
>
> James 1:17

Fruit That Is Displayed

Faithfulness, gentleness, and self-control are on a billboard that displays your character to the world. Your faithfulness displays your endurance, while your gentleness displays your self-control. As the world views the billboard they drive by daily, the message will sink in that your character is built on a strong foundation and does not waiver at circumstances or any wave of doctrine. Your outward display of the fruit of the Spirit will draw the world to the gospel.

Faithfulness—Faithfulness is one of the premier characteristics of God. God does not change. He is forever faithful to His Word. As a born-again believer, you have the fruit of the Spirit within you and the ability to be faithful. Faithful in your marriage, faithful in your finances, and your faithfulness to the house of God are all characteristics that will attract the unbeliever to God. Nobody wants to associate with an unfaithful person who does not keep their word, who ignores appointments, responsibilities, and commitments. The lack of this one part of the fruit being manifested in the lives of some Christians has caused many to reject God because they associate the commitment of His children as an extension of His commitment.

> **He who is faithful in what is least is faithful also in much.**
>
> **Luke 16:10**

> **Moreover it is required in stewards that one be found faithful.**
>
> **1 Corinthians 4:2**

Gentleness—Gentleness should never be confused with weakness. A well-developed athlete with large muscles and great strength can still be gentle. Having the physical strength or the ability to destroy, but having a heart of gentleness will allow a person to experience the tenderness of life and the tenderness of the Spirit of God. While every Christian has been given authority over all the power of the enemy, we must be tenderhearted in our dealings with each other.

> **Finally, all of you be of one mind, having compassion for one another; love as brothers, be tenderhearted, be courteous.**
>
> **1 Peter 3:8**

> **Take My yoke upon you and learn from Me, for I am gentle and lowly in heart, and you will find rest for your souls.**
>
> **Matthew 11:29**

Self-Control—God did not create mankind as robots who would live their lives according to His plan without a choice. God wants us to love Him and obey Him as an act of our own free will and has imparted within us the ability to completely control ourselves and our destinies. Not only does this part of the fruit of the Spirit tell us that God is not controlling us, but likewise, the devil is not controlling us, nor is any other living being or spirit.

While some people have relinquished their self-control to another person or cult, it was ultimately their own choice. A person may be physically enslaved in a relationship and a prisoner under the physical control of someone else; however, no one can control their character but them. Paul addressed this in the Scriptures when he said whether you are slave or free (Colossians 3:9), there is no excuse for not walking in love, kindness, patience, goodness, and self-control.

We have been given total control over our own selves and thus cannot blame anyone, physically or spiritually, for our actions. While some want to be controlled by the Spirit of God, actually God wants us to be led by His Spirit and to be obedient by our own choice.

If you are willing and obedient, you shall eat the good of the land.

Isaiah 1:19

I call heaven and earth as witnesses today against you, that I have set before you life and death, blessing and cursing; therefore choose life, that both you and your descendants may live.

Deuteronomy 30:19

Earlier as we studied the gifts of the Holy Spirit, we were shown in Scripture where these gifts were distributed by the Holy Spirit to individual people upon His desire and timing. The fruit of the Spirit has already been distributed on the day of your salvation and these nine attributes of the Holy Spirit are expressed outwardly by the desire and will of the individual.

... put on tender mercies, kindness, humility, meekness, longsuffering; bearing with one another, and forgiving one another, if anyone has a complaint against another; even as Christ forgave you, so you also must do. But above all these things put on love, which is the bond of perfection.

Colossians 3:12-14

Connected to the Vine

In John 15:5, Jesus said that He was the true vine and we as Christians were the branches. Our responsibility is to bear fruit. Jesus explained that a branch cannot bear fruit of itself unless it is connected to the vine. Then He goes on to say that neither can we bear fruit unless we are connected to Him.

In the same way that a tree limb withers away and no longer bears fruit when it is cut from the trunk of the tree, likewise without being connected to Jesus we cannot live and manifest fruit.

Most people have seen an apple tree. An apple that is ready to eat hangs from the branch, ready to be harvested. But let me ask you this. Have you ever seen an apple growing off the trunk of a tree? No, of course not! That's because it's the job of the branch to bear fruit.

As Christians, we know that the fruit of the Spirit is in all goodness, righteousness, and truth (Ephesians 5:9). While Galatians 5:22-23 gives a more detailed description, the fruit of the Spirit is the by-product of being a Christian that is connected to the vine.

The source of all goodness, righteousness, and truth is Jesus. Jesus said, *"I am the way, the truth and the life"* (John 14:6). Love, light, and life flow from the vine through us and into the fruit. In the fruit are seeds. The seeds continue to grow and multiply in the lives of others. When a Christian stays connected to Jesus and walks in goodness, the fruit produced can change the world.

Jesus made a very interesting statement in John 15:8 that is often overlooked. He said that the way the Father is glorified is by the abundance of fruit that grows from the branches. Walk in the fruit of the Spirit and glorify God.

Abide in Me, and I in you. As the branch cannot bear fruit of itself, unless it abides in the vine, neither can you, unless you abide in Me. I am the vine, you are the branches. He who abides in Me, and I in him, bears much fruit; for without Me you can do nothing... By this My Father is glorified, that you bear much fruit.

John 15:4-5,8

Don't Let the Enemy Spoil Your Fruit

Satan continually attempts to spoil the fruit of the Spirit in you, and he uses people. Several years ago, I was the worship leader at a denominational church. I loved it. To lead people in worship was a joy and I always tried to present myself as a joyful leader. It's easy when you love to worship Jesus. Joy is almost automatic.

After church one Sunday, my wife and I were eating at a local restaurant when one of the long time members of the church came into the restaurant with her husband. They walked over to our table and began to talk. She said, "This morning at church as you were leading worship, I could see that you were happy and enjoyed what you were doing." I smiled and was feeling really good. I thought I was getting a compliment. Then she went on. "And that just disgusts me to no end."

She said, "When Jesus entered a town, He walked in with six disciples flanked on the right and six flanked on the left. He didn't smile and He certainly didn't lift His hands and look happy when He sang." At first I thought she was joking, because the first thought that came to my mind was the image of Wyatt Earp and Doc Holliday at the gunfight at the O.K. Corral. But I could tell by the look on her face she was serious.

While I was allowing the joy of the Lord to flow through me during the praise and worship service and later at the restaurant, the enemy had devised a plan to steal my joy. He used the words of a church member to do it. At that point, I had a choice to make. I was in control of my destiny. Would I become offended and hurt by the words spoken to me and the attitude of this church lady, or would I recognize that it was just an attack and let it go? She made several more demeaning comments, but as she left the restaurant, I put a smile on my face and we actually laughed about it.

In the years that have passed, I have often looked back on the attempt of the enemy to steal my joy that day and realized how insignificant his attempt was. The attacks of the enemy will always be insignificant if we do not allow them entrance into our heart. We can focus on the sadness of the world on the outside and the problems and emotions that go with them, or we can focus on the promise that is on the inside. Focusing on the problems brings despair, but focusing on the promise brings joy.

While some may wonder how we can keep calm in a situation like this and not react with harsh words, we need to remember the fruit of the Spirit that is within us contains self-control. And when these nine attributes of the Spirit are manifest in our lives, our responses to every situation will be godly and bring victory.

We Have the Victory

Years ago, I attended the final game of the World Series. The game was intense and the crowd was really into it. But when the final out was made, I observed a distinct difference between the two dugouts. The team that had won was having a victory celebration. They were leaping on each other, jumping up and down, and having a great time, while in the dugout of the losing team, there was great sadness.

Where there is victory, joy is automatic. As Christians, we must know we are victorious! The way things look should never change what we know. If things look bad, we can still have joy because we know the truth and the truth is Satan has been defeated and we are on the winning team (2 Corinthians 2:14).

A Witnessing Tool

As a Christian, your best witnessing tool is your ability to walk in the fruit of the Spirit. If you will live your life walking in love, joy, peace, kindness, and self-control, others will be attracted to you and to what you have. They will be drawn to you and desire what you have that has created this lifestyle.

Jesus put it this way: *"Let your light so shine before men, that they may see your good works and glorify your Father in heaven"* (Matthew 5:16). If you will live your life walking in the fruit of the Spirit, the light of the gospel will shine from you and the Father and His Word will be illuminated.

Theological debates and the reasoning of man are not what bring the lost to Christ. It is the light shining in the darkness that is the result of a Christian walking in the fruit of the Spirit.

CHAPTER 18

QUENCHING THE SPIRIT

Do not quench the Spirit.

1 Thessalonians 5:19

In this passage, the Greek phrase for *do not quench* is *mē sben-nyte*. The same root word for quench is used in Ephesians 6:16 where we are told that our shield of faith will quench the fiery darts of the enemy. While it is true that the fiery attack of the enemy is to be eliminated, Paul instructs the church that the fire of the Holy Spirit should never be quenched.

To help with understanding what "quench the Holy Spirit" means, here are some other biblical versions of First Thessalonians 5:19:

"Don't put out the Spirit's fire." (GOD'S WORD Translation)

"Don't stifle the Spirit." (Holman Christian Standard Bible)

"Do not stop the work of the Holy Spirit." (International Children's Bible)

"Do not smother the Holy Spirit." (Living Bible)

"Do not extinguish the Spirit." (New English Translation)

"Don't try to stop what the Holy Spirit is doing." (New International Reader's Version)

"Do not hold back the work of [stifle; quench; extinguish] the Holy Spirit." (Expanded Bible)

"Do not quench [subdue, or be unresponsive to the working and guidance of] the [Holy] Spirit." (Amplified Bible)

One of the shortest verses in the Bible is *"Do not quench the Spirit,"* and it has a warning that must be heeded. Even though it is just a few words, if you don't heed it, it will change your whole theology. Ignoring this warning of quenching the Spirit can cause you to miss the source of the true power of God and thus eliminate the source of your deliverance. To quench the Spirit is to reject God.

By quenching the Spirit, portions of the Bible have to be ignored or explained away using methods that do not rightly divide the Word. Through my many years of ministry, I have heard explanations of Scripture that made absolutely no sense whatsoever because the person attempting to explain Scripture had a "quench the Spirit" mind-set.

Are Tongues Forbidden in the Church?

When addressing praying in the spirit and the gift of tongues, Paul said that we should desire prophecy—to hear the Word of God. But in the same verse, he also said we should not forbid anyone to speak in tongues.

> **Therefore, brethren, desire earnestly to prophesy, and do not forbid to speak with tongues.**
>
> **1 Corinthians 14:39**

In this statement Paul is telling the leadership in the congregation that they should not forbid someone else to speak in tongues, but he then addresses the individual who would be praying in the spirit or operating in the gift of tongues. Because the spirit of a person is subject to them and because through the fruit of the Spirit we have self-control, the one receiving the gift or praying in the spirit must allow all their actions to be done decently and in order.

Let all things be done decently and in order.

1 Corinthians 14:40

Quenching by Rejecting God's Gift

Do not quench the Spirit. Do not despise prophecies. Test all things; hold fast what is good. Abstain from every form of evil.

1 Thessalonians 5:19-22

Once while ministering at a meeting in Illinois, the power was present to heal. This meeting was well attended and I particularly enjoyed the praise and worship. The style could be best defined as Southern Gospel. The lady who played the keyboard was in a wheelchair. Although her legs were paralyzed, her hands were definitely anointed. I could close my eyes and almost picture myself at a church in Mississippi or Louisiana.

That particular night I related several testimonies of healings I had observed. When it came time for ministry, someone took the lady who was playing the piano and started wheeling her towards me. There were many people who came forward for ministry that evening and while I was ministering to others, the lady who had played the piano stood out of her wheelchair and began to walk around the auditorium. Someone later told me they could "feel the electricity in the air." While they may have felt something physically, it was actually the Holy Spirit imparting His gifts. The room did seem electrified and many people received healings that were outwardly verifiable.

Later, I asked one of the local pastors who was in attendance about the lady who played the piano. I was excited that she had gotten up and walked around the auditorium. With great confidence, she walked as though she had never been in a wheelchair. The pastor replied that after walking around the room for about ten minutes, she sat back down in her wheelchair and her friends wheeled her out. He said, "She hasn't walked since. It appears as though she lost her healing."

Of course, this troubled me and I wondered why someone who had been healed and able to walk out of a wheelchair would return and sit back in it again. It was not an audible voice, but I heard the Holy Spirit speak to my heart and tell me, "Some people reject the things of God even after they have tasted of them, and for some they reject the things of the Spirit and return to what's comfortable." I also learned that while some people quench the Spirit before they receive, others, through ignorance or laziness reject the Holy Spirit even after He has imparted a gift for them.

While the gift of healing was distributed to me, the one who was to receive it, rejected it. Quenching the Spirit can be done on two levels. The Spirit can be quenched by the person who is ministering the gift, or the Spirit can be quenched by the person who is to receive the benefit of the gift.

Hindering the Move of God

I am currently the president of an international ministers association. I have always felt the call to minister to ministers and especially to train and assist young men and women who are entering the ministry.

One belief that I have that could be somewhat controversial is the belief that every minister who is truly called of God should have full control of what they teach and preach and should never be ruled over by the doctrines of man that would be contradictory to doctrines of God.

Many years ago, I was assisting a pastor who was called of God and who had an idea that I believe was inspired by the Holy Spirit on how to reach the people in his community. Without getting into the details of this plan, the bottom line is it was going to cost several thousand dollars. While the church did not have a lot of money in the bank, it had enough to accomplish what was on the pastor's heart. I sat and watched as he poured out his vision to the men who were running the church and to my utter astonishment, I heard one man say, "You may be hearing from God, but we just don't feel that we should do this project at the present time."

How sad when a man who is called of God and hears direction from God is forced to submit to the control of local businessmen. Because they have been given a place of authority in a ministry, they can override the one who is called.

It is true that as Christians, whether we are in the ministry or not, we are to submit ourselves to each other and we are never to be above correction (Ephesians 5:21). However, we must be able to walk in freedom to do the will of the Holy Spirit without having to submit to the pride, greed, or earthly wisdom of man.

Quenched by the Logic of Man

Another time as a young man, I sat in a church business meeting where the church was deciding whether to spend $5,000 on a bus to pick up some children who had no way to go to church because their parents did not attend. The parents, however, were willing to send the children. The church had $30,000 in their savings account and had been saving it for quite a number of years. $30,000 may not seem like a lot for a church to have in its savings account by today's standards, but many years ago for a small church in a small town, that was a large amount.

The pastor, who was wanting to have the bus and the bus route to bring the children to church, explained that this would be a good way to get some young people saved. But a gentleman, who had been in the church all of his life and obviously ran the church board, said, "Yes, we know that a few young people might get saved, but I feel we should save the money and not get involved in this project." In my mind I was wondering, "What in the world are they saving the money for?" The church was over 100 years old, the building was paid for and up to date, but greed and their personal security was more important to them than the salvation of a few young people.

Any time that we allow the logic of man to override what the Spirit of God wants done, we quench the supernatural possibility of a miracle.

Making Time for the Spirit

I have attended churches that have predetermined before the worship service starts that the gifts of the Holy Spirit would not be allowed to function in that service. I have heard the excuse given: "Because we are on television, we cannot allow it."

Another pastor told me, "We have a schedule and we don't have time. Sometimes the gifts of the Holy Spirit take up the entire service."

While yet another minister took me to a place of amazement when, just before entering the auditorium, he asked me to not move in any of the gifts of the Holy Spirit because he didn't want to scare people away from his church.

How ridiculous and foolish these statements are. Why would anyone gather together for a service to worship God, but then restrict God Himself from speaking words of deliverance to His children through His Spirit?

Be Led by the Holy Spirit

Another way of quenching the Spirit is attempting to force the Spirit. Actually that cannot be done. There is no power in the universe that can make the Holy Spirit do what He doesn't want to do.

Moving in the anointing and the gifts of the Holy Spirit is an exciting experience. There is no equivalent on earth to the feeling of having the Spirit of God manifest Himself through the believer. It causes a type of euphoria that cannot be achieved through earthly accomplishments or even drugs. There is nothing that physically compares to the freshness of the Holy Spirit in action.

A move of the Holy Spirit is for the purpose of changing lives. In the same way that the purpose of a fuel station is to fill the tank of an automobile so that it can travel great distances, the purpose of the automobile is not to be filled with fuel. While filling the automobile with fuel is necessary for travel, the travel itself is the purpose.

Likewise, the manifestation of the Holy Spirit is for the purpose of living and preaching the gospel to the world. Just before His ascension, Jesus said that His followers would receive the power of the Holy Spirit and He went on to say that as a result, they would be witnesses in Jerusalem, Samaria, and to the uttermost parts of the world (Acts 1:8).

It is the power of the Holy Spirit who lives in us and fills us and empowers us to walk in the fruit of the Spirit and receive the gifts of the Holy Spirit. The Holy Spirit causes our light to shine the goodness of God to the world and the result is God is glorified. Receiving and moving in the things of the Spirit are for the glorification of God, not for the glorification of man.

Let your light shine before men in such a way that they may see your good works, and glorify your Father who is in heaven.

Matthew 5:16

Because of the freshness that comes through the moving of the Spirit of God, there have been those who have attempted to force the Holy Spirit to manifest Himself by physical and mental manipulation. While it is true that we can create an atmosphere for the Holy Spirit to manifest Himself as He wills, He doesn't "show up" because we imitate a previous manifestation.

I have been in meetings where the Holy Spirit was manifested in unique ways and it was truly a great move of the Holy Spirit where people received personal ministry. The very next night, the same people with the same ministers arrived at the same building and attempted to have the same move of the Holy Spirit. While to the casual onlooker the two meetings may have seemed similar, one was led by the Holy Spirit and the other was simply a manipulation of the crowd through their emotions and desires.

It is extremely important to always be led by the Spirit and to not allow fleshly manipulation to actually quench something that the Holy Spirit may be wanting to do that was different from the night before. True spiritual maturity is led by the voice of God and not by the desires of the flesh. We should never be led by the popularity of a minister or the size of a ministry, but always be led by the Holy Spirit.

Do Not Grieve the Spirit of God

**Do not grieve the Holy Spirit of God, by whom you
were sealed for the day of redemption.**

Ephesians 4:30

You cannot separate the deeds of the flesh from the work of
the Spirit. Paul clearly tells us that when we lie to our neighbor, when we steal, and when we speak evil, we grieve the
Holy Spirit. Just as clearly he states that when we are kind to
one another, tenderhearted, and forgiving that it pleases God.
Simply stated, when you speak evil, when you have anger,
wrath, and bitterness (having an attitude), it grieves the Holy
Spirit of God.

**Let all bitterness, wrath, anger, clamor, and evil
speaking be put away from you, with all malice. And
be kind to one another, tenderhearted, forgiving one
another, even as God in Christ forgave you.**

Ephesians 4:31-32

When you grieve the Holy Spirit, you hinder His ability to minister through you. We grieve the Holy Spirit by
lying, having fits of anger, stealing, and using corrupt speech.
(Ephesians 4:25-29.) In other words, our relationships with
others and how we treat them affects our relationship with
the Holy Spirit. When we sin against others, we sin against
Him and that grieves the Holy Spirit. Remember, when
Ananias and Sapphira thought they were lying to Peter, they

were actually lying to the Holy Spirit and the result was devastating. (Acts 5:1-10.)

Other believers are also a part of the body of Christ, just like you are. When you are offensive to them, you are offensive to Him. The Holy Spirit is looking for a conduit He can flow through that is not blocked by the sin that grieves Him. We cannot live a lifestyle of yielding to the flesh and expect the Holy Spirit to use us to do His work.

Throughout the Scriptures we are told what God likes and what He doesn't like. Likewise, we are told what pleases Him and what displeases Him. But when it comes to the Holy Spirit, His Spirit, we are given specific commands. These are not suggestions; neither are they just good ideas. We are clearly told, do not grieve the Spirit of God and do not quench the Holy Spirit.

CHAPTER 19

GOD IS SPIRIT

God is Spirit and those who worship Him must worship in spirit and in truth.

John 4:24

The Bible clearly tells us that God is Spirit. The Holy Spirit is the Spirit of God and the Holy Spirit is God. When we describe the Spirit of God, we are describing the essence of God Himself. Although God reveals Himself to man in three different manifestations, He is *Yod Hey Vav Hey* (Hebrew). In heaven He is the Father, on earth He was the Son, in us He is the Holy Spirit, and eternally these three are one.

In the Old Testament era, the Spirit of God dwelt inside the ark of the covenant on earth. Men traveled to the tabernacle or temple in order to worship God Almighty. But now and for all eternity, the body of Christ is the temple of the Holy Spirit. We no longer have to go to a place, but we are the place.

When we receive Jesus as our Lord and Savior, we receive the Spirit of Jesus. The Holy Spirit and the Spirit of Jesus is the same Spirit (John 17:22). As Christians, we have the

257

Spirit of God, the Spirit of Jesus, the Spirit of Christ, the Holy Spirit living in us. They are different names but the same Spirit.

While our spirit is contained in our body, the Holy Spirit is there also sealing us until the day of redemption (Ephesians 4:30). Through this indwelling, we have direct communication with God.

Names and Descriptions of the Holy Spirit

There are different names and descriptions given to the Holy Spirit in the Bible. They reveal His work on the earth and the character of God.

The Seven Roles of the Holy Spirit—Comforter, Counselor, Helper, Intercessor, Advocate, Strengthener, and Standby. *"And I will ask the Father, and He will give you another Comforter (Counselor, Helper, Intercessor, Advocate, Strengthener, and Standby), that He may remain with you forever — "* (John 14:16 AMP).

The Spirit of Truth—*"The Spirit of truth, whom the world cannot receive, because it neither sees Him nor knows Him; but you know Him, for He dwells with you and will be in you"* (John 14:17).

The Helper—*"But when the Helper comes, whom I shall send to you from the Father, the Spirit of truth who proceeds from the Father, He will testify of Me"* (John 15:26).

The Holy Spirit of Promise—*"In Him you also trusted, after you heard the word of truth, the gospel of your salvation; in whom also, having believed, you were sealed with the Holy Spirit of promise"* (Ephesians 1:13).

The Spirit of Wisdom and Understanding, the Spirit of Counsel and Might, the Spirit of Knowledge and the Fear of the Lord—*"The Spirit of the Lord shall rest upon Him, the Spirit of wisdom and understanding, the Spirit of counsel and might, the Spirit of knowledge and of the fear of the Lord"* (Isaiah 11:2).

He Indwells Believers—*"If the Spirit of Him who raised Jesus from the dead dwells in you, He who raised Christ from the dead will also give life to your mortal bodies through His Spirit who dwells in you"* (Romans 8:11).

Our Guide—*"However, when He, the Spirit of truth, has come, He will guide you into all truth; for He will not speak on His own authority, but whatever He hears He will speak; and He will tell you things to come"* (John 16:13).

Our Seal and Guarantee—*"God... has sealed us and given us the Spirit in our hearts as a guarantee"* (2 Corinthians 1:22).

Intercessor—*"Likewise the Spirit also helps in our weaknesses. For we do not know what we should pray for as we ought, but the Spirit Himself makes intercession for us with groanings which cannot be uttered. Now He who searches the hearts knows what the mind of the Spirit is, because He makes intercession for the saints according to the will of God"* (Romans 8:26-27).

Teacher—*"These things we also speak, not in words which man's wisdom teaches but which the Holy Spirit teaches, comparing spiritual things with spiritual. For 'who has known the mind of the Lord that he may instruct Him?' But we have the mind of Christ"* (1 Corinthians 2:13,16).

The Spirit of Grace—*"Of how much worse punishment, do you suppose, will he be thought worthy who has trampled the Son of God underfoot, counted the blood of the covenant by which he was sanctified a common thing, and insulted the Spirit of grace?"* (Hebrews 10:29).

The Spirit of Life—*"For the law of the Spirit of life in Christ Jesus has made me free from the law of sin and death"* (Romans 8:2).

The Spirit of Holiness—*"Jesus was declared to be the Son of God with power according to the Spirit of holiness, by the resurrection from the dead"* (Romans 1:4).

The Spirit of Glory—*"If you are reproached for the name of Christ, blessed are you, for the Spirit of glory and of God rests upon you. On their part He is blasphemed, but on your part He is glorified"* (1 Peter 4:14).

The Spirit is a Witness—*"The Spirit Himself bears witness with our spirit that we are children of God"* (Romans 8:16).

Author of Scripture—*"For prophecy never came by the will of man, but holy men of God spoke as they were moved by the Holy Spirit"* (2 Peter 1:21).

The Spirit of Wisdom—*"That the God of our Lord Jesus Christ, the Father of glory, may give to you the spirit of wisdom and revelation in the knowledge of Him"* (Ephesians 1:17).

The Spirit of Adoption—*"For you did not receive the spirit of bondage again to fear, but you received the Spirit of adoption by whom we cry out, 'Abba, Father'"* (Romans 8:15).

The Spirit of the Father—*"For it is not you who speak, but the Spirit of your Father who speaks in you"* (Matthew 10:20).

The Spirit of His Son—*"And because you are sons, God has sent forth the Spirit of His Son into your hearts, crying out, 'Abba, Father!'"* (Galatians 4:6).

God—*"But Peter said, 'Ananias, why has Satan filled your heart to <u>lie to the Holy Spirit</u> and keep back part of the price of the land for yourself? While it remained, was it not your own? And after it was sold, was it not in your own control? Why have you conceived this thing in your heart? <u>You have</u> not <u>lied</u> to men but <u>to God</u>'"* (Acts 5:3-4).

The Spirit of God—*"The earth was without form, and void; and darkness was on the face of the deep. And the Spirit of God was hovering over the face of the waters"* (Genesis 1:2).

The Promise—*"Behold, I send the Promise of My Father upon you; but tarry in the city of Jerusalem until you are endued with power from on high"* (Luke 24:49).

The Spirit of the Lord God—*"The Spirit of the Lord God is upon Me, because the Lord has anointed Me to preach good tidings to the poor; He has sent Me to heal the brokenhearted, to proclaim liberty to the captives, and the opening of the prison to those who are bound"* (Isaiah 61:1).

Eternal Spirit—*"How much more shall the blood of Christ, who through the eternal Spirit offered Himself without spot to God, cleanse your conscience from dead works to serve the living God?"* (Hebrews 9:14).

The Power of the Highest—*"And the angel answered and said to her, 'The Holy Spirit will come upon you, and the power of the Highest will overshadow you; therefore, also, that Holy One who is to be born will be called the Son of God'"* (Luke 1:35).

The Spirit of Prophecy—*"And I fell at his feet to worship him. But he said to me, 'See that you do not do that! I am your fellow servant, and of your brethren who have the testimony of Jesus.*

Worship God! For the testimony of Jesus is the spirit of prophecy''' (Revelation 19:10).

Spirit of Christ—*"But you are not in the flesh but in the Spirit, if indeed the Spirit of God dwells in you. Now if anyone does not have the Spirit of Christ, he is not His"* (Romans 8:9).

As we can see from the above list, it is amazing and remarkable the number of ways the Holy Spirit reveals Himself to us. He is the anointed power of God for our deliverance in every area of our lives. Jesus has paid the price with His blood and through His grace, this awesome power of God is available to us. While many are waiting for God to move, God is waiting for us to apply our faith and when we do, the door is opened for the Holy Spirit to do His work.

CHAPTER 20

UNDERSTANDING THE MYSTERIES OF GOD

The mystery which has been hidden from ages and
from generations, but now has been revealed to His
saints.

Colossians 1:26

G od is eternal. He has no beginning and He has no
end. For countless eons of time God existed without
there being a universe. Before the galaxies existed, there was
God. Everything that we see had a beginning. There was a
day that God spoke and all that we know appeared. However,
before the Word proceeded from His mouth, the cosmos was
non-existent.

By the word of the Lord the heavens were made, and
all the host of them by the breath of His mouth. For
He spoke, and it was done; He commanded, and it
stood fast.

Psalm 33:6,9

At the writing of this book, science tells us that our known universe is 64 billion light years in radius. As man's ability increases, science is discovering there is no end to space. Although man is coming to this knowledge, he is unable to comprehend the limitlessness of the knowledge he has attained.

Science has never been able to disprove the existence of God, nor has it been able to disprove His Holy Scriptures. While some ridicule and some proclaim their lack of belief in a Supreme Being, the truth is that it only takes a few moments of observation to know all that exists is not some type of cosmic accident. There must be a Supreme Intelligence that formed and created our world.

The reality is this. It takes more faith to believe that the earth and the daily lives of mankind somehow just mystically evolved from space dust, than the faith required to believe in intelligent design.

Daniel's Prophecy

When God inspired men to write the ancient Scriptures, He revealed Himself, His purpose, and His plan for mankind. The prophet Daniel was told to shut up the words and seal up the book until the time of the end. Then he was told that one of the signs of the end times would be that many would run to and fro and that knowledge would increase (Daniel 12:4).

The last century has shown the greatest increase in travel and knowledge in all of the history of mankind. In the 6,000 years that man has been on the earth from Adam until the

1900's, man traveled at the speed of the fastest animal he could find. But within the last century, man has gone from traveling 100 miles in a day to thousands of miles per hour traveling through space.

Knowledge is being accumulated through observatories and science labs at such a high rate, it has been estimated that at the writing of this book it would take over twenty years for all of the data that has been collected to be reviewed. Truly the words in the ancient writings of Daniel are true. The end times will be defined as rapid travel and increase of knowledge. We are in these times now and according to Scripture, the knowledge hidden from the ages is to be revealed to the people of God (Colossians 1:26).

Understanding the Deep Things of God

Throughout my years of theological study and as a pastor, I have encountered countless people who have the attitude that the knowledge of God can never be understood by man. They commonly use phrases like, "You just never know what God's going to do." Of course, that is not true. God clearly tells us what he's going to do, what He wants us to do, what He likes, and what He doesn't like. God's plans and purposes for man are only a mystery to those who are afflicted with spiritual laziness.

In Paul's letter to the Corinthians, he quotes a statement from the Old Testament where it says, *"But as it is written: 'Eye has not seen, nor ear heard, nor have entered into the heart of man the things which God has prepared for those who love Him'"* (1 Corinthians 2:9).

While he is actually quoting from Isaiah (Isaiah 64:4) and while this may have been true for the Old Testament saints who were living before the Promise was given on the Day of Pentecost, it is not true for the New Testament believer. And Paul clarifies this in the very next verse by continuing, *"But God has revealed them to us through His Spirit. For the Spirit searches all things, yes, the deep things of God"* (v. 10). So as a believer we cannot say that we do not know what is in store for us unless we quench the Holy Spirit and restrict Him from giving us the revelation He desires to give us.

When Jesus was talking to His disciples after His resurrection, He reminded them that the words He used when He was teaching them about Himself had to be fulfilled because they were written in the law of Moses and the Prophets and the Psalms. Then He supernaturally opened their understanding so that they could comprehend the Scriptures.

> **Then He said to them, "These are the words which I spoke to you while I was still with you, that all things must be fulfilled which were written in the Law of Moses and the Prophets and the Psalms concerning Me." And He opened their understanding, that they might comprehend the Scriptures.**
>
> **Luke 24:44-45**

This same Spirit who lives in every believer wants to do the exact same thing today. He, by His Spirit, wants to open our understanding so that we can comprehend the mysteries of the Scripture.

Interesting Stories or Revealed Truths

Once, while talking to a large group of people, Jesus ended His speech by saying this, *"He who has ears to hear, let him hear!"* (Mark 4:9). Later when He was alone with His twelve disciples, they asked Him about the teaching that He had given to the people. He told them they had been given the ability to know the mystery of the kingdom of God because they were with Him and followed Him. But to the other people who were non-believers, His sayings would just be parables or interesting stories. (Mark 4:10-11.)

This principle illustrates how someone can read the Bible and share stories such as Noah and the Ark, David and Goliath, Jonah and the big fish, the feeding of the five thousand, etc. and only see these events as parables or interesting stories while at the same time a Christian, by the revelation of the Holy Spirit, can see beyond the superficial story and grasp the deep mysteries as revealed truths. The world can't do it because the world is not led by the Spirit. But a Christian who allows the Holy Spirit the opportunity to teach and reveal will obtain untold depths of understanding. The revelations of the mysteries of God are without end.

Protection from Deception

When Paul was writing to the Christian believers in Rome, he told them he did not want them to be ignorant of a specific mystery. He goes on to say being ignorant of the mystery would make them wise in their own opinion (Romans 11:25).

He was telling them not to give up the wisdom of God and try to substitute it with the wisdom of man.

Many times in Scripture, Paul made the statement that he did not want his followers to be ignorant (Romans 11:25; 1 Corinthians 12:1; 2 Corinthians 1:8; 1 Thessalonians 4:13). The root word of ignorant is "ignore." By ignoring something, you become ignorant of that subject. If a student in school ignores algebra, then they will be ignorant concerning algebra. Likewise, if you ignore the mysteries of God by quenching the Spirit and having an "it really doesn't matter anyway" attitude, then the Scriptures will not be revealed to you and you will be susceptible to false teaching.

I come from a large family. My mother was one of twelve siblings and my dad was one of four which meant I grew up with a lot of aunts and uncles and dozens of cousins. But a few years ago, one of my aunts, along with her daughter (my cousin) started attending a Bible study held by a very charismatic man. After a period of time, this charismatic leader convinced many women to leave their husbands and move away with him. My aunt and my cousin were two of them. This made national news and eventually the federal marshals caught up with this group and justice took its course.

My aunt and my cousin were rescued and today my cousin and her husband are working in a successful ministry.

But here's the point. Unless a person is grounded in the Word of God and has the Holy Spirit revealing the truth, then a person can become susceptible to unscrupulous teachers who can lead them astray for their own purpose. In fact, this is exactly what the Word of God predicts will happen in the last days. Being grounded in the Word is your protection from deception.

> But you, beloved, remember the words which were spoken before by the apostles of our Lord Jesus Christ: how they told you that there would be mockers in the last time who would walk according to their own ungodly lusts. These are sensual persons, who cause divisions, not having the Spirit.
>
> Jude 1:17-19

Hidden Mysteries Revealed to the Saints

When Paul was writing to the church in Ephesus, he told them that they had been redeemed through the blood of Jesus and forgiven of their sins according to the riches of His grace. He went on to say that Jesus had abundantly given them all wisdom and prudence (common sense and good judgment) by revealing to them the mystery of His will. The mysteries of His will are not hidden from the church, but are available by the Spirit. (Ephesians 1:7-9.)

Paul then summed up everything concerning the mysteries of the kingdom of God in Colossians 1:26 where he said these mysteries that had been hidden throughout the ages and hidden from generations have now been revealed to His saints. The Holy Spirit is not a mystery, but His purpose and desire have been revealed to the born-again believer of Jesus Christ.

> The mystery which has been hidden from ages and from generations, but now has been revealed to His saints. To them God willed to make known what are the riches of the glory of this mystery among the Gentiles: which is Christ in you, the hope of glory.
>
> Colossians 1:26-27

Once the Holy Spirit moves inside of us when we are born again, He will abide with us forever. That's good news. You will never be separated from God because He will eternally live in you!

The Secret Place

> Now to Him who is able to establish you according to my gospel and the preaching of Jesus Christ, according to the revelation of the mystery kept secret since the world began but now has been made manifest, and by the prophetic Scriptures has been made known to all nations, according to the commandment of the everlasting God, for obedience to the faith.
>
> Romans 16:25-26

God has kept secrets for us, not from us. He's kept the mysteries and now, He is revealing these mysteries to us. It's called progressive revelation. As we get closer and closer to the time when Jesus comes back to get His church, we are going to have more and more revelation of these mysteries.

Of course, the mysteries of God cannot be fully comprehended by the reasoning of carnal men.

But the natural man does not receive the things of the Spirit of God, for they are foolishness to him; nor can he know them, because they are spiritually discerned.

1 Corinthians 2:14

There are many things God has kept secret for us and it is our responsibility to obtain these secrets. Once we understand them, they are ours. We can claim them.

If we want God to give us those secrets, then we have to know where He keeps them hidden for us. Jesus told us about it in Matthew 6:6: *"But you, when you pray, go into your room, and when you have shut your door, pray to your Father who is in the secret place; and your Father who sees in secret will reward you openly."* Go into the secret place of your prayer closet. That doesn't have to be with the brooms and the mops. It is where you go to get alone with God and to get into His presence.

Psalm 91:1 says, *"He who dwells in the secret place of the Most High shall abide under the shadow of the Almighty."* If you are under His shadow, you are in His presence. So the secret place is in the presence of God. That's where you are going to get the answers to the mysteries. That's where you are going to get the secret things of God revealed to you.

I want to tell you something about the presence of God, the secret place. There are no limits in the secret place. God will take you beyond what you can ask or think (Ephesians

3:20). When you spend time in the secret place in the presence of God, He will reveal His secrets to you. You have to make a quality decision to practice that each day. Practice spending time in His presence.

"I will give you the treasures of darkness and hidden riches of secret places, that you may know that I, the LORD, who call you by your name, am the God of Israel" (Isaiah 45:3). I believe that this verse has a two-fold meaning. First of all, in the last days God is going to transfer the wealth from the wicked so that we will receive the treasures of darkness and the hidden riches of the secret places (Proverbs 13:22). And secondly, when God is referring to the hidden riches of the secret places, He is talking about the mysteries of the kingdom—the secret things that He has hidden for us for this day and time.

The secret place is an awesome place. You can go in there discouraged and come out uplifted. You can go there confused and come out not confused any more. You can know exactly what you should be doing. Go there depressed, and come out full of joy. Spending time in the secret place is vital. We need to get an established heart. Psalm 112:8 says that the man or woman who learns to trust the Lord has an established heart. We need to learn to rely on Him and move when He speaks. He wants to take us to levels where we have never been before.

CHAPTER 21

THE ANSWER TO EVERY QUESTION

For as many as are led by the Spirit of God, these are sons of God.

Romans 8:14

Within the mind of God is the answer to every question. With His voice He speaks all knowledge and wisdom. His Spirit is the power to solve every problem known to man.

Through my many years of ministry, I have been asked countless questions. People are always looking for an answer, a solution, to their problems. Sometimes the question is spiritual, sometimes it's financial, and sometimes it has to do with relationships. Although I have heard thousands of questions, I have come to this conclusion. There is one answer to every question and it is simply this. Be led by the Holy Spirit.

As a Christian, when we train ourselves to hear the voice of God and to submit to the Spirit of God, there will be no mountain left unmoved, there will be no problem unsolved, and we can walk in the freshness of His glory.

When the enemy attacks and it looks like there is no way of escape, then quit looking at the circumstances. Quit listening to the lies of the enemy. Listen for the voice of the Lord as He speaks to you through His Holy Spirit and His Word, and the victory will be yours.

God is the God of creation. Through His Word the universe was created and by His Spirit, the church is empowered to be the hands of the Lord on this earth and the voice that speaks the gospel until our Lord returns.

How to Receive the Holy Spirit

When Jesus was on the cross, He made a profound statement when He said, *"It is finished"* (John 19:30). All of the work that He had been sent to do by His Father had been completed. He preached the gospel to the poor, He healed the brokenhearted, He proclaimed liberty, He healed the blind, and He defeated the work of the enemy. Three days after His crucifixion, He was resurrected by the Spirit of God (Acts 10:40) and He placed His blood on the altar in heaven. When His blood touched the altar, it completed the work of God and put into motion the continuing plan of God for the salvation, cleansing, and deliverance of man. At the moment the sacrificial Lamb of God placed His blood on the altar, all the work had been completed and man could receive Jesus as Lord and Savior by the simple act of confessing with his mouth the Lord Jesus and believing in his heart that God raised Him from the dead.

If you confess with your mouth the Lord Jesus and believe in your heart that God has raised Him from the dead, you will be saved. For with the heart one believes unto righteousness, and with the mouth confession is made unto salvation.

Romans 10:9-10

This may sound too easy, but that's because it is. All the work that needs to be done for a person to receive salvation (everlasting life) is to receive the work of the Lord Jesus. God loved us so much that He paid the ultimate price of sacrificing His Son so that all who receive His Son as Lord and Savior will be saved. John 3:16 says that God loved us so much that He sent His Son, so that whoever would simply believe in Him would not perish, but have everlasting life. He did the work and all we have to do is receive His gift.

This is the grace of God. We could not save ourselves. We did not have the ability or the power to receive everlasting life, but God did. Because of His love, He empowered us with His grace and gave us the opportunity to choose life.

For by grace you have been saved through faith, and that not of yourselves; it is the gift of God.

Ephesians 2:8

What Do I Do Now?

Believing and receiving is the method God has implemented for a Christian to receive everything that God has to offer. Receiving the baptism of the Holy Spirit is no different. Jesus

275

clearly explained that the heavenly Father would give the Holy Spirit to those who asked.

If you are a Christian, you have the Holy Spirit living inside of you. Everyone in the upper room on the Day of Pentecost was a Christian and the Holy Spirit was living inside of them. They had already believed that God had raised Jesus from the dead and they had already been confessing it with their mouths, but a second experience occurred in the upper room and they received a power they didn't have before. You can receive the same power in the same way. Jesus did not lie. He spoke the truth when He said if you ask the Father to give you the Holy Spirit, He will give you His Holy Spirit.

If you then, being evil, know how to give good gifts to your children, how much more will your heavenly Father give the Holy Spirit to those who ask Him!
Luke 11:13

If you are a Christian who desires to be filled with the Holy Spirit, then all that remains is for you to ask and receive. You may ask, "But how do I receive the baptism of the Holy Spirit?"

First of all, do not put God in a box and limit Him. In the Bible, the Holy Spirit was received several different ways. When Paul came to Ephesus, he encountered a group of believers that had not even heard of the Holy Spirit. After briefly teaching them, he laid hands on them. Immediately, the Holy Spirit came upon them, and they spoke with tongues and prophesied. (Acts 19:1-7.)

Another time, while Peter was preaching at Cornelius' household, the Holy Spirit fell upon those listening, and apparently it was totally unexpected (Acts 10:44).

On the Day of Pentecost, the 120 in the upper room were waiting and expecting when they were filled with the Holy Spirit (Luke 24:49).

While all three of these events were different in nature, everyone received the same Holy Spirit and the same manifestation. So the answer to this question is the answer to every question. Be led by the Spirit. If you ask the Father to fill you with His Spirit, He will.

Believe and You Will Receive

Personally, I received the Holy Spirit at a Bible study in my home when I asked a man of God to lay hands on me to receive. I have seen hundreds receive the Holy Spirit during church services and others have told me of how they received the Holy Spirit alone at home. But the common denominator of all of these accounts is this. They asked believing they would receive, and they received.

While the manifestation of tongues is not always immediate for some believers, the manifestation of tongues will happen. Don't quench the Spirit. Relax and receive.

I'll See It When I Believe It

The world has the attitude of "I'll believe it when I see it," but we cannot allow this into our spiritual thinking. As Christians, we are to walk by faith and not by sight (2 Corinthians 5:7).

This simply means that we believe what God says instead of believing what we see or hear from the world. If God says one thing and our feelings reveal something different, we believe what God says and reject our feelings. For Christians, "We'll see it when we believe it."

This principle also applies to receiving the Holy Spirit. While there will be manifestations that take place after the Holy Spirit is poured out upon us, we must never forget that it is the Holy Spirit we receive and the manifestations follow. There are some teachers who place so much emphasis on the manifestation, they do not believe someone has received the Holy Spirit until they see a manifestation of tongues.

But if Jesus said if you ask the Father, He will give you the Spirit and you ask the Father for the Spirit, then you have received His Spirit. How do we know we have received? Because we have asked and God promised that if we ask, we would receive. When we can rest in His promise that His Word is true, the manifestations will follow.

I have known Christians who have come to the altar to be filled with the Holy Spirit service after service and year after year and they wonder why they have never seen a manifestation of tongues. The answer is quite simple. They haven't received the manifestation because they haven't believed they have received the Holy Spirit.

We must never forget that we must seek His kingdom and His righteousness first and then the things (the manifestations) are given (Matthew 6:33). This is a foundational principle in the kingdom of God.

The Bottom Line

As Christians, we must choose to be led by the Spirit instead of yielding to the flesh. The flesh will lead you into deception because it is subject to the senses and the lies of the world, but the Spirit will lead you into truth (John 16:13). It should be obvious for a Christian to be led by the Spirit. The Bible says life and death, blessing and cursing, have been placed before us, and after making this statement, we are told to choose life.

> **I call heaven and earth as witnesses today against you, that I have set before you life and death, blessing and cursing; therefore choose life, that both you and your descendants may live.**

> **Deuteronomy 30:19**

Receiving Jesus as your Lord and Savior is an experience that changes your destiny for all eternity. The Holy Spirit moves inside of you and brings with Him the fruit of the Spirit that enhances your life. Receiving the baptism of the Holy Spirit as a second experience releases the power that Jesus promised. This power will bring supernatural abilities through the gifts of the Holy Spirit.

The price for all of this has been paid in full. There is nothing left for you to do except to believe and receive. Do not quench the Spirit, but receive the fullness of everything God has planned for you.

As you have read this book, you have discovered the awesome power of the Holy Spirit and you know that God has placed His Spirit inside of you for all eternity (John 14:16).

There is no being or power in the universe that can come close to the power that is within you. By the blood of Jesus you have been given the authority to exert this power over the enemy and you have been promised that nothing by any means shall harm you (Luke 10:19).

God is light and in Him there is no darkness (1 John 1:5). We are children of the light (Ephesians 5:8) and have been given authority by our Father. When we receive the baptism of the Holy Spirit and allow Him to impart His gifts to us, our light will shine in a dark world.

Through the power of His Spirit, we will fulfill the commission He gave to the church (Matthew 28:19). We must never forget the parting words of our Lord and Savior Jesus Christ, *"You shall receive power when the Holy Spirit has come upon you"* (Acts 1:8).

BIBLIOGRAPHY

Carter, Howard. *Questions & Answers On Spiritual Gifts.* Tulsa: Harrison House, Inc., 1976.

Graham, Billy. *The Holy Spirit.* Nashville: Thomas Nelson, 1988.

Hagin, Kenneth E. *The Holy Spirit and His Gifts.* Tulsa: Rhema Bible Church, 1991.

Sumrall, Lester. *The Gifts and Ministries of the Holy Spirit.* New Kensington: Whitaker House, 1982.

PRAYER OF SALVATION

God loves you—no matter who you are, no matter what your past. God loves you so much that He gave His one and only begotten Son for you. The Bible tells us that "...whoever believes in Him shall not perish but have eternal life" (John 3:16 NIV). Jesus laid down His life and rose again so that we could spend eternity with Him in heaven and experience His absolute best on earth. If you would like to receive Jesus into your life, say the following prayer out loud and mean it from your heart.

Heavenly Father, I come to You admitting that I am a sinner. Right now, I choose to turn away from sin, and I ask You to cleanse me of all unrighteousness. I believe that Your Son, Jesus, died on the cross to take away my sins. I also believe that He rose again from the dead so that I might be forgiven of my sins and made righteous through faith in Him. I call upon the name of Jesus Christ to be the Savior and Lord of my life. Jesus, I choose to follow You and ask that You fill me with the power of the Holy Spirit. I declare that right now I am a child of God. I am free from sin and full of the righteousness of God. I am saved in Jesus' name. Amen.

If you prayed this prayer to receive Jesus Christ as your Savior for the first time, please contact us on the Web at **www.harrisonhouse.com** to receive a free book.

Or you may write to us at
Harrison House • P.O. Box 35035 • Tulsa, Oklahoma 74153

The Harrison House Vision

Proclaiming the truth and the power

Of the Gospel of Jesus Christ

With excellence;

Challenging Christians to

Live victoriously,

Grow spiritually,

Know God intimately.

Fast. Easy.
Convenient.

For the latest Harrison House product information and author news, look no further than your computer. All the details on our powerful, life-changing products are just a click away. New releases, E-mail subscriptions, testimonies, monthly specials—find it all in one place. Visit harrisonhouse.com today!

harrisonhouse

Lord God!

What is the gospel?

Is Just salvation — spiritual life

Is Just Healing ← physical life
                                  Mental life

It also your ⟹ Economic life
                                or
                             well being

What is the gift of Adminstration & Government?

THE NINE GIFTS OF THE HOLY SPIRIT
- THE THREE GROUPS -

THE GIFTS OF SPEECH
They say something
- Prophecy
- Different kinds of tongues
- Interpretation of tongues

THE GIFTS OF POWER
They do something
- Faith
- The working of miracles
- Gifts of healings

THE GIFTS OF REVELATION
They reveal something
- The word of wisdom
- The word of knowledge
- Discerning of spirits

LOM
LARRY OLLISON MINISTRIES

THE PARALLEL FLOW OF THE SPIRIT

THE GIFTING FLOW Received by the will of the Holy Spirit (1 Corinthians 12:4-11)	NATURAL FLOW Activated by your own will
THE GIFT OF THE WORD OF WISDOM	**WISDOM** *If any of you lacks wisdom, let him ask of God, who gives to all liberally and without reproach, and it will be given to him. (James 1:5)*
THE GIFT OF THE WORD OF KNOWLEDGE	**KNOWLEDGE** *Be diligent to present yourself approved to God, a worker who does not need to be ashamed, rightly dividing the word of truth. (2 Timothy 2:15)*
THE GIFT OF FAITH	**FAITH** *So then faith comes by hearing, and hearing by the word of God. (Romans 10:17)*
THE GIFTS OF HEALINGS	**HEALING** *Is anyone among you sick? Let him call for the elders of the church, and let them pray over him, anointing him with oil in the name of the Lord. And the prayer of faith will save the sick, and the Lord will raise him up. (James 5:14-15)*
THE GIFT OF THE WORKING OF MIRACLES	**MIRACLES** *Whatever things you ask in prayer, believing, you will receive. (Matthew 21:22)*
THE GIFT OF PROPHECY	**PROPHECY** *Then Philip went down to the city of Samaria and preached Christ to them. (Acts 8:5)*
THE GIFT OF DISCERNING OF SPIRITS	**DISCERNING OF GOOD AND EVIL** *...Those who by reason of use have their senses exercised to discern both good and evil. (Hebrews 5:14)*
THE GIFT OF DIFFERENT KINDS OF TONGUES	**PRAYING IN THE SPIRIT** *For he who speaks in a tongue does not speak to men but to God, for no one understands him; however, in the spirit he speaks mysteries. (1 Corinthians 14:2)*
THE GIFT OF INTERPRETATION OF TONGUES	**REVELATION OF THE WRITTEN WORD** *These things we also speak, not in words which man's wisdom teaches but which the Holy Spirit teaches, comparing spiritual things with spiritual. (1 Corinthians 2:13)*

Spirit of Wisdom and Understanding

SPIRIT OF HOLINESS

Spirit of the Father

Spirit of His Son

Standby

Eternal Spirit

The Promise

Spirit of Glory

COUNSELOR

TEACHER

INDWELLS BELIEVERS

Spirit of Prophecy

INTERCESSOR

SPIRIT OF KNOWLEDGE AND THE FEAR OF THE LORD

HOLY SPIRIT

Spirit of Truth

Our Guide

SPIRIT OF LIFE

Helper

Spirit of God

Comforter

Our Seal

Spirit of Christ

Power of the Highest

Author of Scripture

God

OUR GUARANTEE

Spirit of Adoption

Holy Spirit of Promise

Spirit of Grace

WITNESS

STRENGTHENER

Spirit of Counsel and Might

Intercessor

Advocate

Spirit of the Lord God

Spirit of Wisdom